EDUCATION BRINGS SOCIAL ADVANTAGES

JOHN LOK

Copyright

Contents

Preface

Introduction

Our social economic development whether it can develop in success, it depends on many factors. They may include: employment rate increasing factor or raising productivities factor, high consumption factor, traveler leisure need factor. However, I believe that educational industry will be the main factor to influence any countries can have long time economic development in success.

In my this book, I shall attempt to explain why and how educational development will be the main factor to influence any countries can develop their economy to achieve long time success. Readers can make analysis to judge whenter education industry development is the main factor to cause any countries to develop their economy in success.

Prologue

Table of content

CHAPTER ONE

Outsourcing educational and economic development strategy

● Outsourcing educational development strategy

Lesson learning teaching method

It is nowadays, social learning combines face-to-face and online teaching into one learning experience popular teaching method, e.g. distance learning. What is lesson learning teaching method ? It means that methodology is the way(s) in which teachers share information with students. The information itself is known as the content, how that content is shared in a classroom is dependent on the teaching methods. There are five methods of teaching? Their levels may be from low to high teaching methods. They may include: from low teaching level, such as direct instruction, kinesthetic learning, differentiated instruction to high teaching, expeditionary learning, personalized learning and game-based learning teaching level.

What is teaching modeling? Modeling means after telling

students what to do, it's important to show them exactly how to do it, e.g. how to correct mistakes, how to give feedback to let student to know how to correct mistakes, why the student has mistakes, how one group students can have cooperative learning attitude more easily, how to achieve experiential learning.

How to let students feel interest to learn in led classroom or class discussion? How to give inquiry-guided instruction to let student can feel adapt to learn in classroom easily. All of these methods are very important to influence every student learning attitude in order to achieve easy learning aim or raise their learning interest to improve teachers' teaching performance.

What are four teaching styles? In the contemporary classroom five distinct teaching styles way include: As the primary strategies adopted by modern teachers, they include the authority style, delegator style, facilitator style demionstrator style and hybrid style. IN classroom, teachers can learn any one of these four styles in order to teach students more easily. The term teaching method refers to the general principles and management strategies used for classroom instruction. Any teacher choice of teaching mthod depends on what fits him/her, his/her educational philosophy, classroom demographic subjects (areas) and school mission sratement.

Hence, a effective teaching method comprises the principles and methods, used by teachers to enable student learning. What of implementation in teaching is to enable the learners to take intelligent interest in the lession. Hence, in this category of methods, both the teacher and the learners have to fit into the content that is taught. Discussion may be used in the classroom for the purpose of lesson development. For exmaple, a lesson plan is the instructor's road map of what students need to learn and how it will be done effectively during the class time, the teacher needs to weight student individual assessment tasks and the different teaching methods. Then to make decision, whether which is their best teaching method for diverse learners, for example the demonstrator is a lot like the lecturer, but their lessons include multimedia presentations, activities and demonstrations or another teaching method may be to record results, take ohots/ videos or simply as a behavior management technique.

Hence, a teaching strategy is the method, the teacher uses to convey information to his/her students who are visual learners too, his/her needs to clearly state his/her lesson goals or objectives for different subjects in order to raise students learning interest. The teacher can follo different personal style teaching method to teach different personal style teaching method to teach his/her students, e.g. authority style means that it is primary used ina lecture or auditorium setting, whereby the teacher will give a lengthy one-way discussion on a pre-assigned topic when students take notes and memorise key pieces of information. It is a formal authory teaching style. Teachers who have a formal authority teaching style tend to focus on content.

This style is generally teacher-centered, where the teacher feels responsible for providing and controlling the flow of the content and the student is expected to receive the content. Another teaching style is depegators style, for subjects that necessitate group work, peer feedback, or lab-based learning, a delegator or group style of tutoring is often adopted. As a delegator, the teacher may take on observer robe to promote collaboration and encourage peer-to-peer learning in classroom. It is helpful to think of teaching styles according to directing, discussing and

delegating. In general, the directing style promotes learning through listening and foolowing directions, the discussing style promotes learning through interaction, and the delegating style promote learning through empowerment.
Another teaching style is facilitator style, teachers adopt a facilitator or activity-based style encourage self-learning in the classroom through increased peer to teacher learning, unlike the lecture style, teachers ask students to question rather than simply have the answer given to them. The teacher's main role is as afacilitator, there to offer support and necessary teaching of skills, when he/she feels students can like he/she ask any questions to let them to attempt to give any possible reasonable answers. It is one exciting and encouraging teaching method.
The another teaching style is demonstrator style, it likes the lecture or authority style of teaching, the demonstrator retains authority in the classroom. However, instead of relying solely on a verbal lecture, the demonstrator style combines lecturers with other teaching forms, including mult-media presentation, demonstrations and classroom activities. The final style is hybrid in classroom, hybrid is a method of teaching that utilizes technology to create a variety af learning environments for students. Instructors who emply hyrid intentionally incorporate technology tools both to enhance student learning and to respond to wide range of learning preferences.
How teacher teachs hybrid classes. It create activities that encourage student interaction and collaboration, discussion forums on class material/topics, online group projects that support collaboration and achieve learning, for example have small groups edit a wiki together, invite students to share their learning opinions and experiences or feeling. So, in a hybrid model, when students are kept

out of school for multiple days, week, or every other week, a sizable percentage of them are likely to interlink or intercontact with other children and adults. So, hyrid learning is a way of experiental learning objectives, and digital course delivery that emphasizes using the best option for each learning objective.

Why any one teacher needs to know whether which teaching style is the most suitable to him/her to apply to teach students, because teaching styles are linked to a teacher's educational value system, and stem from his/her philosophy of education. Being aware of his/her own teaching style (for styles) can help him/her improve his/her teachining methods, and encourage student engagement and ultimately, student outcomes. Hence, any teacher ought need to spend time to learn whether which teaching style is suitable to him/her to teach his/her students in order to let students can raise learning interest and improve examination results or his/her teaching perofrmance in classroom.

Human development policy

Human development policy is belong to educational strategy. The current economic crisis has affected all aspects of life resulting in political instability, personal financial troubles and a growing number of business bankruptcies. How to use effective human development educational policy to prevent the economic crisis threats. I shall indicate that governments ought to consider these different aspects of human development educational strategy to prevent the economic recession crisis occurrence to threaten to influence whose social economic growth.

On the human development educational strategy hand,

examples of which include high quality education and health systems aspects. Different country's government ought to concern, due to it can support the productivity of an economy by providing healthy and highly trained individuals. Because of the country has good human development strategy, then it can use talent labors to assist its economic growth and good governance practices by governments easily. It seems that human development educational strategy, good governance and economic growth has close relationship, so it can reduce the economic recession during times of crisis occurrence. It means that human development can influence economic growth. Economic development implies both the improvement of people's health education and general well being and the presence of positive economic indicaties, such as economic growth and low unemployment with economic development, people will have better education and healthcare and be more productive. Better human development nations tend to have lower crime rates and greater political strategy than less human development nations.

Whether is it a consequence of human development educational strategy to prevent economic recession? It will be an important resource to influence economic growth. How does this human development public educational policy solve economic crisis? Can government use fiscal policy, such as human development to assist economic stabilization to promote growth and the increase of the capital income efficiency? A key issue relates to the effect of how to use public expenditure and its financing to spend human educational development on effects of fiscal policy by using a time series approach.

A general model that includes expenditure on education

and health, which influences human capital, expenditure and health administration, public investment and transfers and consumption of public products four kinds of expenditure. The model can be used to explore and impact of human development expenditure is used on long run per capita income. So, the public expenditure on the long run per capita income can be explored for low, lower, middle and upper-middle income countries policy that is needed to be esimated how to spend for each aspect of human development expenditure to assist to every country's economy development.

What is time series perspective on economic growth to pursue for growth and human development strategies.

A time series perspective on economic growth may be more useful to pursue for growth and human development strategies. A time series can allow to pursue time series studies for particular countries or country groups at particular stages of economic growth. It can allow for a more specific micro behavior of economic agents. In general, any country has three income groups, such as low income, lower-middle income and upper middle income groups. Also, any country may have these four types of public expenditure for human development which including: enhancing education and building up of human capital, public investment to finance general market and subsistence production, e.g. transportation system, such as roads, bridges, harbors, water supply, sanitation, health and care and education.

A 2005 year study had been carried by Dimonson, Marsh & Staunton, which performed an analysis is stock returns in 53 countries, going back to 1900 year for 17 countries, did not find evidence of a significant long term positive relationship between GDP growth rates and equity returns.

Also the analysis from Schroders Economics team found that over the past sixty years, there has tended to be a positive relationship between GDP growth and equity market returns during the recovery, expansion and slowdown phases of the traditional business cycle.

This relationship has traditionally broken down during the recession phase. The Schroders economics team also indicated a traditional business cycle model, which has four stages. In the beginning, it is slowdown stage. It means output above trend, growth decelerating and inflation rising. Next is recession stage. It means output below trend, growth developing, inflation falling. Then, it is recovery stage. It means output below trend, growth decelerating, inflation falling. Finally, it is expansion stage, it means output above trend growth accelerating, inflation is rising.

The economic team also suggested the traditional business cycle model: In the slowdown stage, GDP growth is positive, but falling, inflation is high and rising, so policy strategy is tight recommended in the recession stage, GDP growth is negative and falling, inflation is falling. So, policy strategy is loosening recommended. In the recovery stage, GDP growth is negative and rising, inflation is low and falling, so policy strategy is loose recommended. Finally, the expansion stage, GDP growth is positive and rising, inflation is rising, so policy strategy is tightening recommended. It seems that governments ought concern the business cycle period to evaluate themselves country GDP growth to achieve the most effective policy to adopt to achieve different human development educational (strategies)policies to invest to present economic recession crisis occurrence. Usually, in the recovery and expansion phases of the business cycle, the stock market tends to perform well as rising GDP and earnings growth drives positive excess returns on equity. In the slowdown phase, inflation is still high and monetary policy remains tight, resulting in difficult environment for corporations. It can reduce earnings and stock valuations tends to result in negative excess returns for equities: declining GDP growth is therefore usually matched with poor equity performance. It also explained that during the recession phase, there is often GDP growth is falling, but the excess return on equity tends to be positive. Historically, falling inflation and an accompanying loosening of monetary policy is needed to rise re-rating. Thus, it seems the business cycle and human development educational policy has close relationship. During in the slowdown stage, GDP growth is positive, but falling, inflation is high and rising, then the country's government ought spend less expenditures to human development because GDP growth is stable growth. Otherwise, during it is recession stage or recovery stage, it means output below trend, growth developing, inflation falling. Then the country's government ought spend more to invest to any human development needs to prepare to raise whose labor productivity and GDP growth. Finally, during the expansion stage, GDP growth is positive and rising, inflation is rising. Then the country's government can spend less expenditures to invest human development. Thus, any country's government ought concern what is whose country's business cycle stage to arrange to spend more or less expenditures to achieve its human development educational policy in different business cycle stages.

What is quantitative evidence to review human development educational policy to reduce the threats from economic recession risk occurrence.

Nowadays, political scientists began to apply quantitative methods to classify and measure human resource educational and outsourcing strategy interactions. In general, any countries' policies that maximize growth are optimal that cares solely about pure " capitalists

I shall indicate how to apply quantitative evidence to review educational and outsoucing policy to reduce the threats from economic recession risk occurrence. In fact, economic or welfare outcomes to changes in regulatory policy has close relationship to be suggested outcome indicate to reduce risk face economic recession occurrence to any countries. Every country government ought design to gather quantitative data to prepare any outsourcing human educational development or/and outsoucing policy implementation to support mutual learning and best practice in different societal and market conditions. The goal is to help countries to build better government systems and implement policies at both national and regional level that lead to sustainable economic and social development.

The critical public policy challenge is to ensure that the expected economic benefits from regulatory changes are both achieved and outweigh any economic cost imposed. I shall indicate evidence on the outcomes of regulatory policies to help policymakers how design regulatory measures that work better. This method is called ''regulatory management''. This regulatory management study suggests some conclusions to any policymakers. Firstly, poorly designed human development or/and outsoucing policy regulation can not raise economic activities and ultimately reduce economic growth. Secondly, it is impossible between a regulatory human development or/and outsoucing policy change and the impact on economic outcomes, such as economic growth is from statistic method easily. Third, the reliance on economic recession analysis to investigate the relationship across countries between regulatory variables and economic outcomes may not be readily applicable to any countries and may not always be expressed in economic values. It is particularly useful in developing countries regulatory human development and/or outoucing policy measures for recommendation to policymakers only. Fourth, most quantitative studies deal with the costs of human development and/or outsourcing strategy regulation and give little or no attention to quantifying the benefits of regulation.

For the policymaker, it is important to compare the estimated costs of human development and/or outsourcing regulation. Any policy regulation is intended to correct market failures and assist to economic efficiency and growth. The public policy aims to reduce socially unacceptable income and wealth distributions or it can satisfy expectation that the public should have access to certain products and services, e.g. health care and education irrespective of ability to pay, such as merit products. Some of human development or/and outsoucing strategy regulation, that governments need to concern, e.g. of property rights, company law, law of contract etc. and regulation can provide important economic and social, including environmental benefits. Of course, those benefits need to be set against the costs. Because regulations are the operations of effective economies and societies to market rules, firm's outsoucing and human development strategy e.g. law of contract and protecting property rights and the rights of citizens. It seems regulatory management is important to influence any policies can be achieved effectively, due to one good regulation can supervise the firm leader's behavior and otherwise one bad regulation can not supervise the firm leader's behavior, even it can not assist the country economic growth for long term. So, any firm leader needs to concern how to use quantitative evidence to review human development or/and outsoucring strategy policy if who hopes whose policy's regulations are achieved effectively.

At the same time, economic, environmental and welfare pressures raise the demand for regulation above minimum needed for operating a market economy to prepare to face the economic recession occurrence. So, evidence on the outcomes of outsoucing and/or human development strategy regulatory policies should help policymakers design regulatory measures that work better. Similarly, evidence on the success or failure of regulation can be used for public accountability purposes. Regulatory human development or/and outsoucring strategy policy is defined as the process by which government, when identifying a policy objectives, decides whether to use regulation as a policy instrument and proceeds to draft and adopt a regulation through evidence based decision making. The human development or/and outsoucing strategy shall commit governments to remain a regulatory management system, articulating regulatory policy goals, and the impacts of regulation on competitiveness and economic growth. For example, one firm human development and/or outsoucing strategy regulation, such as employment law or competition law, the regulation of employment law is applied to control any employers' behaviors to give the fair treatment to whose employees and to protect employees' benefits. Besides the regulation of competition law is applied to control the fair competition in market.

Why this human development and/or outsourcing strategy

regulations has direct relationship to economy growth. An identifiable economy theory of specific regulatory policies, e.g. administrative simplification and specific economic and welfare outcomes, e.g. high economic growth. The result is a series about the impact of regulatory management on economic indicators. There can be set out as a causal. Thus regulation can be supportive of market transactions and may result in significant economic, social and environmental benefits. At the same time, ill-designed regulation can have appreciable economic costs, leading to the concept of regulatory burden. In particular, good regulation can reduce the chance of lower economic growth or GDP occurrence, damage investment and competitiveness. But, it has also weakness, such as regulatory costs may act as a barrier to entry into industry in the form of set up cost, e.g. installing equipment to meet health and safety laws and on going annual cost, e.g. preparing returns and facilities inspections.

However, human development and/or outsourcing strategy regulatory can be unduly costly to comply with administrator and enforce, but it simplification can reduce the regulatory burden. For example, regulation may not only affect the behavior of those targeted by a rule (direct effects), but invoke behavioral change in the economy (indirect effects). Whether regulation can support governments to avoid or reduce the threats of economic recession occurrence, it depends on the firm leader's concern how to use quantitative evidence to review human development and/or outsourcing strategy policy before who decides to implement which kinds of regulatory management methods.

In recent year, some countries' firms and/or governments had considered how to achieve human development and/or outsourcing strategy policy field with a view to introducing better regulation. The aim is to ensure that regulation occurs only when it does improve social welfare and that regulatory changes do, so with the minimum net cost or maximum net benefit to society. For a policy making perspective, it is important to appreciate how and why a regulatory achievement can be expected to result in a particular impact.

Causal chain analysis is a technique for explaining the way in which a caused regulatory results in an economic impact. By helping to understand the how and why questions of the firm which needs to decide outsourcing and/or human development strategy, regulatory impact, so causal chain analysis can provide policymakers, with relevant information on the consequences of their policy decisions. It seems that human development and/or outsourcing strategy regulation can lead economic improvements, such as higher GDP growth, higher productivity, move business start ups. etc. Due to the causal chain analysis relates to each component separately. So, any decision maker hopes to achieve better regulation, who needs time to attempt to different regulations to achieve whose policies every year. Then, who can review why whose policy can not improve whose country's economic growth as well as to attempt to find reasons how to apply better human development and/or outsoucring strategy regulatory to achieve better policy to improve its country's economic growth. It seems review regulatory policy which ought to concern to any decision maker, if who wanted to achieve better regulatory policy to raise economic and welfare gains every year.

In capitalism view, capitalism tends equal systematically, through not uniformly to reward business behaviour ,such as human development and/or outsoucing strategy that is honest, fair civil and compassionate. When does irrational honesty behaviour influence social economy development? It concerns behavioral economy to individual decision maker whose individual psychology, social psychology into economics. It helps any organization's human development and/or outsoucing strategy policy makers to incentive in market transactions and in response to policy interventions. So, policy advisers are already using the finding of behavioural economy to advantage to public policy, there is nothing about behavioural economy, but for a long time, it has tended to be concerned how the social economic development, particularly in macroeconomy. For example, human development and/or outsourcing strategy policy makers concern of money in nominal rather than real terms in whose how to solve to unemployment. Also, policy makers neglect to recognize how economic motivations apart from those based on rational calculation usually. Most, probably of policy decision makers' decisions to will be drawn out over many days to come, who feels action rather than inaction to any decision immediately, and not as the outcome of a weighted average of probabiities. It seems that the policy decision maker's irrational honesty behaviour will influence how our social's economic development to be good or bad.

Regulatory management method

Whether it has relationship between human development and/or outsourcing strategy political instability and national economic performance. By past history indicated that the depletion of resource ,e.g. human resource and/or business strategy during wars may be one reason why some countries fail to sustain adequate economic growth. However, because economic growth affects a population's well being, this question concerning how was related to growth is important from a policy perspective. So, civil wars can influence any country's economic growth because civil war can cause the falling changes in a country's physical and human capital as well as lacking technology supporting can reduce GDP per capita to be country during war occurs. For example, during civil war does not occur, then trade liberalization, democracy, government stability and a legal system that strongly protects private property rights enhance growth.

Finally, I shall explain why human development behavior, such as honesty has moral consequences to cause economic growth. For citizens of all too many of the different countries, where poverty is still the normal. But the tangible improvements in the basic of life that make economic growth, so important whenever living standards are low, greater life expectancy, few diseases, less infant mortality and malnutritian have mostly been played out long before a country's per capita income reaches the levels enjoyed in today's advanced industralized economy. In fact, immoral or dishonesty business or economic behaviours, such as wrong outsourcing strategy achievement are caused by some business leaders who pursue material well being and who aim to do benefit to themselves, but it will cause illegal money transactions to raise any overall country's economic or GDP growth. In fact, this business transactions are not legal. So, which can't cause GDP or economic growth to any country. Also, the illegal businesses can not contribute any benefits to any society, so which can not bring any economic benefits or welfares to any countries to satisfy any citizen'e needs ensurely. Even, in parts of the world where the need to improve nutrition and literacy and human life expectancy is urgent, there is often aspect to the recognition that achieving superior growth is a top priority.

So, it seems dishonesty human development behaviours will not improve and raise low income level people whose life expectancy and life quality because this illegal businesses income is used to spend to the illegal businesses or immoral policy decision makers themselves benefits and who won't spend to social welfare. It seems that these illegal businesss or immoral policies can not assist any economic growth and raise GDP growth rate as well as dishonesty or immoral economic activities can not bring any benefits to societies in our world, even these bad behaviours will bring harm to our societies. e.g. encouraging illegal drug sale to harm young people health and raising crimes rates; winning illegal gamble to earn illegal profit to increase high interest loan businesses and crimes or causing bad families relationship to raise social challenges.

What is the root of the irrational behavioural problem? I believe that is our conventional thinking about economic growth fails to reflect the breadth of what growth, or its absence, means for any society. There are some people's dishonest behaviours only weigh material positives against moral negatives. I believe this dishonest economic activites are seriously. In some cirsumstances dangerous incomplete, the value of arising standard of living lies individuals live, but in how it shapes the social, political and ultimately the moral character of a people. It seems any organization's wrong human development behavior or wrong outsourcing strategy will influence the country's economy growth.

Economic growth means a rising standard of living for the clear majority of citizens. So, dishonest economic behaviours can only give benefits to the individual and these irrational behaviours can not give welfare to overall societies. In fact, economic growth bears moral benefits as well. So, it seems dishonest behaviours can not raise moral benefit, then it can not also raise economic growth to any country. Moreover, dishonest behaviours are also caused to any country's political democracy. e.g. Many policy decision makers usually only consider self benefit, so who will neglect to consider social welfare benefits to whose citizen. Themselve benefit behaviours will be unfair to whose citizen. The importance of the connection between economic growth and social and political progress and the consequent concern for what will happen of living standards tail to improve, are not limited to the United States and other countries that already have high income and established democracies. So, economic growth or its absence often plays a significant role not only progress from dictatorship to democracy, but also the democracies by new dictatorships.

Also, for dishonest behaviours are caused by decision makers, such as the link between economic growth and social and political progress in the developing countries has yet other political implicatons as well. For example, the continuing absence of political demoracy and basic personal freedoms in China has deeply troubled many observers in the West. Until China gained admisson to the World trade Organization in 2002 year, these concerns regularly gave rise in the Uniter States to debate on whether to trade with China on a most favored nation basis. These concerns still cause questions about whether to give Chinese firms advantage advanced American oil company. Both sides in this debate share the same objective: to foster China's political liberalization. How to do so , however, remains the focus of intense disagreement. The improvement in nutrition, housing, sanitation and transportation has been dramatic, when the freedom of Chinese citizens to make economic choices, where to work, what to buy, when to start a business is already broader than it was with continued economic advance, the average Chinese standard of living is still only one eighth that in the United states, greater freedom to make political choices too, it will probably follow. So the economy is actually developing, like China won't have to wait until China can achieve Western level incomes before they experience significant political and social liberalization.

To conclude, if any country's policy makers who do not consider citizen welfare and who only consider self benefit, it will cause dishonest behaviours to influence social economic development to cause poor situation for long term. So, policy makers must need concern their behaviors arc rational choicc to makc any economic decisions to let their citizen to give welfares for long term. Also any businessmen ought choose to do rational economic behaviours to benefits for societies and clients and governments in order to achieve economic growth to GDP to their countries if who hope whose businesses can be stable to compete for long term. So, policy decision makers and businesses ought consider rational honesty behaviour before who do any economic decision.

Outsourcing educational development policy

How honesty is influenced to economic positive relationship? The dishonesty behaviour includes: e.g. corruption is as an illegal payment to a public agent to obtain a benefit that may or may not be deserved, or the abuse of public office for private gains to consume, corruption probably amounts are to a large share of the gross national product in any countries. So, corruption worries policy makers and international organizations, who remains the adverse effects of corruption.

However, in the macroeconomic view, the academic literature is less definite about how bribes minimize the waiting costs associated with queuing in a equilibrium. Both of those waiting cost associated with queuing and inefficiency models equate bribes as allocating the true worth of the licenses or permit to the most worthy bidder in public sector. Forbidding bribes that amounts to prohibiting the use of price mechanism in the public sector. In terms of economic growth, the only thing worse than a society over centralized, dishonest bureaucracy is over-centralized. So, the quality of government institutions, including the degree of corruption, affects investment and growth as much as other political economy variable. e.g. political freedom, civil liberties and political violence. Another example, some firms that pay more bribes also spend more time with bureaucrats in more corrupt countries and have a higher cost of capital, thus countering the view of corruption.

Finally, some countries are likely are fairer and regulation is less. How does corruption affect income inequality? In addition, capital market imperfection and government spending have been suggested as two channels for corruption to affect inequality and economic growth. Finally, to what extent can corruption explain the differences in inequality and economic growth? So, it seems corruption is associated with a smaller increase in income inequality and a larger drop in growth rates. Also, corruption raises income inequality to a lesser extent in countries to achieve higher government spending. So, it seems corruption dishonest behaviour has close relationship to influence any countries' GDP economic growth.

Corruption is understood as sale of government property for private gain. However, most economists view corruption as a major obstacle to development. It is seen as one of the causes of low income and is believed to play a critical role in poverty. Perhaps the most quoted example of this is speed money paid by business people to government officials to speed up bureaucraties procedures. At the macro level, there is evidence that corruption affects adversely many of the proxy causes of economic growth. e.g. investment in manufactured and human capital. Moreover, high levels of corruption tend to with a lack of political accountability and disrespect for property rights factors which themselves tend to be obstacles to economic growth. More fundamentally, however, there is a sense in which the focus on growth in GDP per capita is misguided. Ultimately, human educational development is about how to improvement in human welfare. However, corruption is developing a few with access systematic distort political and economic decisions which might be made systematically with conflict of interest at play. For example, different countries' banks which achieve different bank schemes to aim to avoid illegal money saving from drug trafficking to cause false economic growth in any countries. The anti-corruption strategy advocated to economic development, democratic reform a strong civil society with access to information and overseeing the state, and the presence of rule of law. The governance program facilities at the request of client governments, a series and surveys involving broad segments of society and national and local government performance.

The causes of its human educational development and many and vary from one country to the next. It seems corruption dishonest behaviours can cause to seem as one country's false economy growth and even, global false economy growth after any illegal economic activities had been done from any illegal businessmen. So corruption is a global issue which is government all over the world. However, what is the causes and consequences of corruption? It is possible that corruption is the intentional with length relationship aimed at deriving some advantage from this behaviour for oneself or for related individuals. So, in micro-economic view, corruption cause is derived from some advantage from this behaviour for the person. Otherwise, in macro-economic view, corruption cause is also derived from some advantage this behaviour for the organization, even overall country's social benefit, e.g. illegal shares buying and selling trading activities, illegal bank saving transaction source from drug trafficking activities.

On human development educational aspect, many of the assumptions which are attempted to rationalize the process of educational development have been criticized or abandon. However, the education quality role of different educational regulation, the choice of financing methods, the examination and certification procedures or various other regulation and incentive structures will influence educational effect to satisfy public needs. Thus, educational policy makers need to satisfy public needs. Moreover, educational policymakers also need to concern any new policy making environment which will seriously constrain their attempts to ensure the early discussion of planning considerations as part of the education policy making process. So, every country's environment factor will influence every educational policymaker's individual decision.

As defined, policy represents decisions that are designed to guide (including to constrain future decisions or to initiate and guide the implementation of previous decisions). It is this time bound nature of policy and of policy making that makes it is such a critical concern for the educational planner. However, the failure of the traditional planning models and the recognition of the lack of nationality that can occur in policy making there combined to create an atmosphere of pessimism among some educationalists.

To capture the details of the decision making process of any educational planning itself, an analytical framework is presented that goes beyond the initial decision point to examine both the preceding actions (contextual assessment, technical analysis and the generation, valuation and selection of policy options) and the subsequent activities (planning and conducting implementation, impact assessment and where appropriate, design). Thus, the framework covers the full policy planning process, but with a focus on the facilitating and constraining effects that policy decisions and how they were derived and have no the choices available to educational planners.

There are two ways of value to educational planners. First, the methodology of the framework and conclusions of the any one of educational case studies should help in the analysis of current educational policies and decision making procedures (an analysis of policy). So, it is a present method to gather current data from current case studies to make the update conclusions to achieve any any of eductional policies. Otherwise, Second, the another framework can be applied to have evaluation of proposed policies and used to forecast policy outcomes and the probability of successful implementation, given the country of fiscal and management capacity, political commitment etc. So, this framwork is a futuer predict educational method to gather data how to get the recommedation to achieve the effiective quality of educational policy in the future.

Educational policies can be lower differ in terms of scope, complexity, decision environment, range of choices and decision criteria. Any educational policy decision deals with large scale policies and broad resource allocation will have these questions to need to answer. For example, on strategic view, how can we provide basic education at a reasonable cost to meet equity and efficiency objectives? On multi program view, should resources be allocated to university level education? On program view, how would occupational training centre be designed and provided across the country? On issue specific view, should graduated of rural universities be allowed to transfer to any one of city area universities to study easily? On the psychological view, some researches indicated behavioral economics with emotions has close relationship to any policy making, such as educational policy. More recently, economists as well as psychologists who are specifically interested in decision making have begun to take greater concerning emotional influence. So, it seems any policy decision making whose any one of final policy decisions which is influenced to achieve or not achieve from their emotion indirectly. Usually, then an economy is doing well, there is less incentive to encourage new entrepreneurial firms if the country's citizens and firms have enough jobs supply and have enough labor supply in the job market. It seems that good economic growth country will have this question why it needs to take a risk on something new. So, emotions have close link to our societies to influence any country's citizens real needs and entrepreneurs‘ business aim to develop any societies' economy to be grown. So, any countries' policies decision makers ought concern whose enterprises and citizens whose real needs, then who can attempt to choose what methods of policies to assist whose countries' economy development more effective.

What is national human development educational policy

However, behavioural economy is not concerned with such normal phenomena, rather it is concerned with consistent patterns of behaviour which depart from rational actor models. The mean may be displaced as when most people under-scare for retirement, or the distribution of behaviour may reflect several modes of behaviour as when users of credit cards who pay in full and those who pay minimum amounts. Otherwise, in terms of public policy, most such departures from rationality have little or no consequence. It is possible to accomodate non-rational behaviour with a set of indifference with a quality, such as non-rational utility, ensuring that all behaviour can be modelled.

Concerning irrational honesty whether this behavior can influence social economic development. I shall indicate those questions to attempt to be considered, such as: Can there be a growing scaraity without a growing shortage or a growing shortage with a growing scarcity? Can a decision be economic if there is no money in involved? Can there be surplus food in a society where people are hungry? For example, building ordinary and building luxury housing both involves using many of the same resources, such as bricks, pipes, and construction labour. How does the allocation of these resources between ordinary housing and luxury housing tend to change after rent control laws are passed? When a government institution or program produces counter productive results, is that necessarily a sign of irrationality on the part of those who run that particular institution or program? Why do American manufacturers of computers or television sets tend to have them transported by others? When Chinese manufacturers tend to transport themselves? How did the movement of population from rural to urban America affect the economy of retail selling in the early twentieth century? Advertising even when it is successful, is often considered to be a benefit only to those who advertise, but of no benefit to consumers, who have to pay the cost of the advertisement in the higher price of the products who buy. Is it irrational economy behaviour to society? Why would luxury hotels be charging lower rates than economy hotels? Whether governments choose to protect competition or protect competitors which method is better? What have been some of the economic and social consequences of the substitution of machine power for human strength, as a result of industralization and the growing importance of knowledge, skills and experience in a high-technological economy? How can per capita income be increasing by 50 % over a period of years, when average family income and average householder income remain almost stable over those same year? Does inequality of income tend to be greater or less in long run than in the short run?

All above questions concern the social and economic influences won't be better if the policy decision makers or businessmen do any irrational honesty behaviours. It seems rational honesty behaviour is important to any policy decision makers or businessmen because whose rational or irrational behaviour can influence social economic development directly are driven to act by economic as well as social ethical and other reasons. So economists need to study of what motivates individual acts, especically regarding economic decisions, offers an intellectual challenge to the human sciences. So, if economists can predict to judge whether any policy decision makers or businessmen whose act is irrational or rational, then who can assist the country's economic development more easily.

On natural environment view, whether every country's natural environment has close relationship to assist its economic growth. The natural environment is central to economic activity and growth, providing the resources, we need to produce products and services and absorbing and processing unwanted by-product in the form of pollution add waste. So, environment assets contribute to managing risks to economic and social activity helps to regulate flood risks, regulating the local climate both air quality and temperature and maintaining the supply of clean water and resources both.

Government's role is to send clear signals and set a long term policy framework in order to provide businesses with the certainty who need to make investments in low carbon and resource efficient technologies. It is also essential that government listens to and works with business, so that policies are designed in a way that avoids unnecessary burdens and removes potential barriers to success. So, the natural environment plays an important role in supporting economic activity. It contributes: directly, by providing resources and raw materials, such as water, timber and minerals that are required as inputs for the production of products and services and indirectly, through services provided by ecosystems including carbon water purification, managing flood risks and nutrient cycling.

The relationship between economic growth and the

environment education is complex. Several different drivers come into play, including the scale and composition of the economy, particularly the share of services in GDP as opposed to primary industries and manufacturing and changes in technology that have the potential to reduce the environmental impacts of production and consumption decisions when also driving economic growth. In fact, economic growth involves the combinations of different types of capital to produce products and services these include; produced capital, such as machinery, buildings and roads; human capital, such as skills and knowledge, natural capital, e.g. raw materials are extract from the earth, carbon and services is provided by forests and social capital, such as institutions and ties within communities. So, government needs to concern that national resources can not be extracted too much to lead our natural capital is lacked to produce any products or to provide services in the future.

In particular, market failure in the provision and use of environmental resources mean that natural assets would be over-used in the absence of government intervention. These market failures arise from the public product characteristics of the natural environment, external costs and benefits, where the use of a resource by one party has impacts on others, difficulties in capturing the full benefits of business investment in environmental research and development, and information failure.

Market failures may include water quality and to vehicle emissions to influence human's body health. So, any countries' government needs to achieve these policies which concerns on environmental protection aspect to achieve its public spending and technology policy, such as on developing flood infrastructure, supporting low carbon technologies electric vehicles. Also on the information provision and other policies to address barriers to influence consumer's behavior change, such as product labelling policies and policies to increase take up of resource efficiency measures to provide environment protection. So, effective environmental policy is likely to require and the use of multiple instruments, each tackling to require part of the problem when avoiding duplication and unnecessary regulatory burdens. Also, pricing environmental inputs can correctly help any businessmen to manage how to use natural resources effectively.

Environmental education policy aims to reduce how the economy and the businesses are to adverse environmental events, by reducing environmental risk both. For example, not just investments that facilities emissions reductions to avoid dangerous climate change, but also those investments that help to economy adapt to climate impacts already locked in by past and current emissions. The natural environment plays a key role in our economy, as a direct input into production and through the many services it provides.

Environmental resources, such as minerals and fossil fuels directly facilities the production of products and services. The environment provides other services that enable economic activity, such as carbon, filtering air and soil formation. It is also vital for against flood risk, and soil formation. It is also vital for our wellbeing, providing us with recreational opportunities, improving our health and much more. Human wellbeing in a complex and diverse concept, determined by a wide-range of factors including levels of income absolute and relative, health status, educational attainment, housing conditions and environmental quality.

National capital contributes to economic output through two main channels: directly as an input to the process of economic activity, indirectly through its effect on the productivity of the other factors of production. However, natural capital is as a direct input to wealth creation, which can provide the raw materials for economic production of products the raw materials for economic production of products and services, it includes non renewable resources like, fossil fuels, minerals metal extracted from the natural environment to produce energy, machinery, consumer products, renewable resources, natural processes or own reproduction. Why do our governments need to concern environmental policy? The reasons include natural areas provide global life support functions, including climate regulation and regulation of the chemical composition of the atmosphere and oceans. When natural areas play a role in the maintenance of life essential services, it is difficult to evaluate and demonstrate the contribution that particular habitat types or areas make. Water regulation can reduce flood and storm protection and prevent damage. Natural processes can also provide water quality benefits, pollution includes the removal of nutrients and pollutants from water, filtering of dust from the air, and providing noise. Waste sink includes all non recycled waste is produced by economic activity. In the absorptive capacity of the atmosphere, the oceans and the soil protection, such as many wetland habitats, provides benefits by preventing soil loss. Nutrient cycling includes storage, processing and acquisition of nutrients essential for plant growth in ecological process and waste decomposition, naturally occurring micro-organisms provide benefits through their ability to break down organization matter and speed up the process of waste decomposition.

Government overseas education outsourcing policy
As the global financial crisis has reminded as once again of the economic role of trust and confidence, social capital attributes which are difficult to influence any policy decision maker's ration decision making more easily. Referring to recent financial crisis, which is related to any psychological drivers of economy activity, we can not understand the economic developments of recent times without psychological insights which go beyond estabished notions of rationality in its economic sense. As peope with weigh the costs and benefits of each possibility. This assumption is based on the expectation that individuals and firms will act in a consistent manner, with a reasonably well defined notion of what who like and what whose objectives are, and with a reasonable understanding of how to attain those objectives.
In fact, behavioural economy is a complement to deductive processes based on those assumptions. In any discipline with practical applications, such as public policy, conclusion is reached by chains of deductive logic based on those assumptions require the test of falsifiability or refutability, or at least that they be supported by confirmatory evidence. However, a rational means the predictive validity of the rational model holds, but that doesn't mean achieving policy should ignore interventions. For example, most people rationally avoid self-harm, but there will be extreme tails of highly protective and of highly reckless behaviour: the latter may require specific protection. So, it seems it has relationship between global financial crisis and individual or organization's irrational behaviour.
How government overseas outsourcing policy can influence on capturing private investment. Can

government overseas outsourcing policy can attract foreign direct investment or different countries? Increased levels of trade and foreign direct investment worldwide, a cause or effect of the closer interdependence of world economies are a reality. What is the relationship among these private, public and civil society sectors? Every country contribution is to add to the public policy stream to understand how the main forces in society operate and cooperate in promoting foreign direct investment. Governments have always been concerned about how to position themselves in an increasingly competitive market for a limited supply of investment resources. Why should a multi-national firm choose one country attraction ? e.g. tax breaks, profit repatriation, low domestic content requirement etc. How can one country strategically outsoucing position itself against others? Is there an association between pro-social public policy and levels of global private investment? We are particularly interested in those economies in earlier stages of development, where pro-social policies are a rarer phenomenon, as they provide a testing for our hypotheses. What is the relationship between the ability of an host country to attract private investment and the quality of pubic policies affecting the life of its citizens? Are pro-social host government policies in host countries linked to higher inward flows of foreign direct investment to that country?

There has three country level macroeconomic indicators to represent different facets of size: Host country economy growth rate, host country population and host country's rate of inflation. GDP growth, the annual percent change of output in real terms percent, reflects the strength of local economy and the increase in the size of domestic market, opening the door to large sales and high profits.

Thus, higher GDP growth should generally be attracted to larger foreign investment. Population is another indicator of market size. It attracted to foreign investment with both large populations and high GDP per capita. So, encouraging immigration and birth rate can attract more foreign investment. Inflation enters the regression as a proxy for macroeconomic stability and as a reflection of the internal or external shocks suffered by the economy during the period under study, which may attract potential inflation sign of internal economic instability and of the host government's inability to maintain consistent monetary policy. It will influence foreign investment confidence. So stable inflation of the host country can increase confidence to let more foreign investment.

How fiscal policy can affect medium to long term economic growth. It is difficult to measure the factors and to determine causality with certainty, between fiscal policy and economic growth relationship. Fiscal reforms are needed to concern structural reforms, e.g. labor or trade and supportive macroeconomic policies. At the macro level, fiscal policy can help to ensure macroeconomic stability, an essential prerequisite for growth at the micro level, tax and expenditure policies can boost growth by altering work and investment incentives, promoting human capital accumulation and enhancing total factor productivity. For example, combining fiscal reforms, e.g. sealing up infrastructure investment when improving the public investment process can increase their effectiveness. Complementary reforms, such as liberalizing trade of fiscal reforms by promoting savings, stimulating investment and not lacking productivity gains, policy uncertainty and high levels of public debt large fiscal deficits reduce aggregate savings in the economy and may lead to inflation, high interest rates and balance of payments pressures, with negative growth consequences. Policymakers need to concern the durability and equity. For example, Netherland, an expenditure cut of 15% of GDP between 1982 year and 2000 year created room sector job-creation. At the same time, both countries managed to avert adverse consequence on income inequality. In advanced and emerging market economies, age related spending on public persons and health care accounts for a large share of government spending (40% and 30%, respectively, IMF, 2014 f). Otherwise, Poland shifted from a financially defined benefit system to an actuarially solvent defined contribution system, and Germany put its pension system on a more sound financial by linking pension benefits to the old age dependency ratio, tightening access to early retirement and rising the statutory retirement age. In health care, Germany and the Netherlands introduced a combination of macro and micro level reforms to contain cost and enhance efficiency, including price controls on pharmaceuticals, higher co-payment and contributions and budget.

National leadership and educational productivity relationship

Whether national leadership and economic growth has close relationship. Leaders have strongest effects in autocracies, where who appear to substantially influence both economic growth and the evolution of political institutions. I shall indicate to explain why substantial roles for individual leaders and national institutional change, which can further influence the growth environment. In the past, examinations of the fundamental causes of growth debate between institutions, culture and geography, which typically operate without reference to the actions of

particular personalities. However, economists may imagine leaders indirectly as policymakers, leaders, themselves educational level are rarely the subject of focus.
The constraints imposed on leaders from electoral pressures, opposition parties, independent legislatures and judiciaries all vary across countries. To the extent that the authority embedded in formal institutional rules and the authority embedded in individuals act as substitutes, the increasing visibility of institutional variation in explaining paths may indirectly motivate leaders' behaviors. Theories of economic growth that emphasize public products, e.g. education, health, public entertainment facilities, such as parks, swimming pools etc. Also, national policies include international trade, monetary policy and fiscal policy etc. or all suggest possibly important roles for a national leader.

However, identifying a causative effect of leaders' educational level on economic growth is challenging. Even, if it has relationship between particular leaders' educational level and particular economic growth in particular economic environment. However, it may be that growth changes drive leadership changes, without a causative effect of leaders' educational level. Assumption that a leader quality is independently, it seems the leader has no influence on economic growth. An important additional assumption is that the leader effects are strongest in autocratic settings, especially in the absence of political parties or legislatures to support the leader's any personal view points to achieve any regulations to influence economic growth effectively. These results point to an important effect between institutions and leader individuals in understanding economic growth paths. However, it seems institutions can influence the impact of national leaders behaviors and that national leaders can also influence the path of institutions. If leaders can influence economic growth, then may further these questions are raised: Do leaders act to obstruct economic growth or do they actively promote it? In this view, leaders can be actively good for economic growth, e.g. by investing in public products, choosing pro-growth trade policies, or overcoming national scale coordination problems. However, related questions of how leaders influence growth are related to the role of national policies in explaining growth. If policies might be well matter, even if leaders do not, if national policies care the expression of broader social forces. So, it seems national policies can also influence economic growth, instead of the leader's personal quality or whose educational level. So, it can get this question and conclusion. When asking how do we make poor countries rich? The unexplained, non-deterministic past of economic growth variation becomes especially relevant and given the results about leadership, more within reach.

Human development outsourcing educational strategy

Promoting honesty in negotiation can influence social economy growth in global. In a competitive and moral imperfect world, business people are often facing with serious ethical challenges. Usually, many businessmen feel justified in engaging in less than ideal conduct to protect their own interests. However, our commonplace that work to promote credibility, trust and honesty of behaviours can influence our social economy growth in long term. For example, deception in negotiation behaviour is immoral, due to success in business typically requires successful negotiations. Given the high value placed on honesty, the incentives for deception in negotiation create a serious moral tension for business people. Not surprisingly, deception in negotiation is a widely discussed problem in business ethics. How many negotiators their views are essentially, who is regarded as a superior moral philosopher, would find them objectionable? For example, philosophical debates about the loss of civilian life in war would be better served by putting resources and intellectual energy into developing political, economic diplomatic and military strategies that resources and intellectual energy how to be chosen to use in military strategies aspect or political aspect or economic diplomatic aspect. The country's leader whose educational knowledge will influence the whole country's social economy development in long term. However, individual and social stability are difficult to maintain in a social setting in which there is serious conflict between ethics and personal welfares. Because irrational honesty behaviour is usually caused between the personal welfare and ethics choice.

Whether behavioral economy can be applied to inform and develop human development or /and outsourcing strategy policy effectively. Such policies stress that changing the way choices are presented or changing the environment in which decisions are made, can substantially alter behavior. Ideas from behavioral economics have helped to develop the traditional economic choice framework, in which people are assumed to make choices that are rational, self interested and consistent. Some of the most important behavioral insights for tax and benefit policy include: Faced with complicated decisions, people may make choices, which are often approximately optimal, in that who maximize welfare, but might in some cases lead to poor choices.

There is evidence that how choices are presented affects

outcomes. The environment in which decisions are made would provide cues to make particular choices or made could provide cues to make particular choices, or some aspects of the choice problem may be more or less influence to consumers. When any policy relates to income and spending, or it is label money for another can affect what people choose to do with it. Individuals appear to care not just about their own outcomes, but also about those of others. This might be because people derive value from fairness and cooperation. These motivations could give intrinsic incentive to make particular choices. It is possible that providing extrinsic incentives, such as taxes, fines or rewards could be crowded our desirable behavior.

Consumers may have to exercise costly self control to make certain choices, such as eating health foods or giving up smoking. Commitment devices to help overcome self control problems are therefore values, for example, raising the cost of tempting choices, increasing cigarette taxes, say: when making choices with uncertain outcomes, people will do a number of behavioral features. Such as, attaching subjective decision weights to each outcome and these may differ from objective measures of probability.

Usually, outcomes are measured against a reference point, relative to the reference point are felt more strongly than equivalent gains. When welfare increases and ever bigger gains falls, as the welfare cost is from ever bigger losses, then people will appear to be risk seekers when welfare cost comes to cause social loss. How people value the future changes with the passage of time. Usually people hope to earn immediate rewards in present than distant rewards in the future. This means that people make plans who find it hard to achieve. People may also make choices under the assumption that their preferences won't change in the future. So, for policymakers those biases have important implications for why behavior change interventions may be necessary.

Behavioral insights provide new reasons to intervene, issues of self control, for example, making failure, where outcomes are come from the perspective of either individuals or society or both usually. As a common failure is the case of externalities, when individual choices generate costs or benefits for others. Since, these are not taken into account in private decision making, which are come from a social perspective, there is too much or too little of the activity. In this case, taxes or subsidies can help private and social incentives. So, behavioral economical concept can be suggested these important insights for externalities, such as private decisions are closer to the social optimum, reducing the need for correcting taxcs or subsidies. It seems that taxes or subsidies will affect to change people's behaviors if social preferences are important. Externalities can arise not just because of how someone affects the well being of others, but also through how decisions made today affect the individual in the future. This is known as an internality. Taxes or subsidies policies both can influence people's present behaviors to be changed and future behaviors will be influenced to be changed from whose present behaviors in societies. Thus, policymakers can not neglect human development or/and outsoucing strategy policy of method to attempt to solve any social challenge nowadays.

Finally, why behavioral economy can assist human development or/and outsourcing policy development. Behavioral economy is a science, includes psychology, economics, finance and sociology to understand human behavior and decision making. Behavioral economics recognizes that constraints in time and mental resources prevent us from optimally evaluating every decision. To deal with our limitations, so we rely on mental decision to judge our face of uncertainty, but we can be leaded to predictably irrational behaviors from behavioral economical concept.

As government agencies enact laws and regulations that are focused in the society. They often rely on restrictions, incentives or public information campaigns in order to change citizen behavior. When well intentioned, those traditional approaches can be accepted. For example, regulations that can be supported to financial advisers disclose conflicts of interest have led to achieve any final results. Disclosures can increase pressures on advisees to comply with the advice provided and in some cases increase greater perceptions of trust rather than the evaluation of biased advice. Similarly, tax incentives can increase retirement savings rates which have had limited impact. Researchers studying the impact of concluded that such policies are an expensive way of encouraging new savings.

On the one hand, governments ought engage their citizens to do any action, whose action is influenced by behavioral economics to discover how behavioral economics can be provided powerful insights into human motivation and behavior. As different countries‘ government experiments are more from academic laboratories to the real world. So, it is a kind of method to be applied to assist any countries' governments how to use effective policy to improve people's lives. For example, designing what is the best reasonable taxes, subsidies, incentives or educational campaigns level at the rate, donations and retirement savings rates as well as healthy food product label consumption of selection etc. strategic policies which are related how to apply behavioral economy to analyze or experiment to gain the better choice among of them.

On the another hand, Economic agents ought attempt to spend time to gather data to choose to do the best decision, but not perfectly national ones. Also economic research should be used reasonable assumptions about agents' cognitive actives. So, economic models should take predictions that are consistent with micro-level data on decisions, including experimental evidence. Moreover, economists ought spend much time to learn from psychologists.

Behavioral economists now routinely combine experimental data, field data and theory to construct their arguments. As behavioral economic continues to gain acceptance, behavioral economists will increasingly find themselves participating in policy discussions. As policy has the ability to do good or to create great mislead, depending on who, leader is in charge of making the rules. Indeed in some cases the findings of behavioral economists suggest that active policies may be quite harmful. Successful policy analysis should be concerned the motives of private actors, e.g. consumers and firms and the public or governmental actors need to design formulate and enforce policy with cooperation to regulators, bureaucrats, politicians. So, human development and/or outsourcing strategy policy analysis must also be carefully concerned the institutional environment in which these private and public actors interact, e.g. , market, elections and bureaucracies. However, any bad decision making is caused from bounded rationality, slow learning, framing and lack of self control with those effects in mind, one might conclude that government can easily improve consumers' welfare by paternalistically helping consumers make better decisions. Such paternalistic policies can improve consumer welfare by enhancing an individual's maximizing whose own welfare. So, this stands in contrast to most public policies, which address externalities or public products problems that arise because of interactions among economic agents.

To conclude, psychology and behavioral economy and public policy which have close relationship to influence human development and/or outsourcing strategy achievement. As if the national leader had health psychology, then who will have more possible to achieve good behavior to perform to decide how to achieve any the best public policies to raise growth to make welfare to whose citizens. So any policymakers ought need to concern how to listen to behavioral scientists to let them to give any recommendation how to improve or review or revise whose psychological challenges to let them have more effort to decide how to choose to do the right decision effectively. Because the relationship between psychology and behavioral science has more generally to influence public policy which is particularly painful and frustrating of the success for any similar policy recommendations. Hence, economics and psychology indeed can provide human development and/or outsourcing strategy policymakers with vital tools to develop the best policy to solve any social challenges.

Consequently, it seems the leader's psychology will influence whose behavioral performance to be decided to choose to do the more correct policy to influence economic development more easily. It also means that one leader's psychology is an important factor to influence any social economic development directly for long term. So who can not neglect to concern whether whose psychological mind is right or wrong to already to make any decisions to plan any policies before whose any polices are implemented. Because the leader's psychology will influence whose behavior is more correct to decide to decide how to do any policies effectively.

Researching the relationship between education and productivity how to influence economic growth in developing Asia countries nowadays, this topic is concerned how to use labor economy method to analyze how to influence education to cause what the macro and micro economic effects are in the developing Asia countries. I shall indicate some developing countries in Asia, e.g. Philippines, Korea, China etc. countries. What the link between education and productivity is? What does the model that characterize key featured of growth processes of Asia countries are? For this topic, I shall suppose human capital is come from such as primary and secondary and tertiary education factor which has a major close relationship to cause the developing Asia countries' economic growth nowadays. My objectives of this research are to explore the relationship between graduates and economic growth, assess what should be the key variable (or variables) of interest and quantify the relationship to developing Asia of some countries.

Human capital has ability and efficiency of labor to transform raw materials and capital into products and services to affect economic growth. The accumulation of human capital improves labor productivity and increases the returns to capital. However, a well educated background is essential to raise technology to develop economic growth in Asia developing countries especially.

In macro and micro economic view, the well educated labor

(human capital) is often as one of the critical factors to influence rapid economic growth to the Asia developing countries' any regions or cities. Because any of these Asia developing countries, such as China, Korea, Philippines etc. countries which need have well educated and knowledgeable labors to raise any employers' productivities and income growth. So productivity and education factor which ought have close relationship to cause the good or bad economic growth in these any one of Asia developing countries. For example, China was an major industrial and farming country between 1960 year and 2000 year. However, after 2000 year, it began to achieve any commercial investment to raise GDP income and to raise more service provision nature of employment chance to domestic labors. e.g. financial investment, shares trading, hotels and tourism and airlines and restaurants and cinemas etc. service nature businesses commercial investment. Moreover, the foreign investors were also attracted to set up factories to manufacture their products in China's country any area locations. It was possible that this foreign investors felt China's workers' wages were more cheaper than themselves domestic worker wages. For example, USA has the minimum wage legislation to protect it's domestic individual worker wage level. Otherwise, China's individual worker wage level is compared to be paid more lower level to compare to USA's minimual legislative individual worker wage level nowadays. It seems China, Korea, Philippines etc. Asia developing countries need have well educated labors to help them to develop economic growth. Because the developed countries' foreign well educated labors, e.g. USA, UK etc. who feel whose countries can give the best salary compensation level and benefits to let them to support to work and to live in whose countries. So the developed countries' well educated labors won't choose to go to China to work very easily. It seems those developing Asia countries which governments need to invest in education sector to increase many knowledgeable human labors capital to assist them to raise whose technological productivity or service productivity or factory productivity to achieve economic growth for long term. If any one of these Asia developing Asia countries still want to keep the competitive position in global environment in the future. So, these Asia developing countries must need good education to train any aspects of high knowledgeable labors to supply to themselves society to work in essential.

Ha, Kim and Lee (2009) provided evidence to indicate that "using panel data covering from 1989 year to 2000 year in Japan, Korea and Taipei, China as the distance to the technology frontier narrows basis research and development (R&D) investment, i.e. highly skilled labor which showed the higher growth effect than development R&D investment , i.e. less skilled labor. They also provided evidence that the quality of tertiary education has a significantly positive effect on the productivity of R&D. Nowadays, education is commonly regarded as the most direct influence to people out of poverty owing to the tendency for employment opportunities especially for higher skilled workers to be created in Asia developing countries. In fact, raising productivity is depended on the quantity and quality of human resource, which itself largely depends on investment in education theoretical linkages between education and growth. Generally, growth theory suggests that economic growth depends on the accumulation of economic, including human assets and the return on these assets, which depend on technological progress, the efficiency which assets are being used. So, growth theory which emphasizes on the centrality of human capital for innovation and technological progress. However, the theory indicates of policy ineffectiveness which characterizes the neo-classical growrh theory by giving importance to the production of new technologies and human capital development. So focusing on factors within the model rather than relying on external factors. It seems the economists of supporting growth believe that improvements in productivity are linked to a faster pace of innovation and extra investment in human capital. Also these economists of supporting growth theory emphasize on the need for governments and private sector educational institutions and job markets for tertiary students‘ demand and to innovate knowledgeable of social economy to actively provide incentives for individual student to become inventive in any countries. They also identify the central role of knowledge as determinant of economic growth. Hence, growth theory can predict positive externalities and spillover effects from development of a high valued-added knowledge economy to the development and maintenance of a competitive advantage across the global.

Why do I research the relationship between education and productivity can influence the economic growth to Asia developing countries? Although, human capital includes education, health and aspects of social capital. The main focus of the present study is on education. The analysis stresses the distination between the quantity of education measured by years of attainment at various levels and the quality measured by scores on internationally comparable examinations, e.g. China education and Korea education comparision. In fact, the global long term economic growth was the central macroeconomic problem and it was fortunately accompanied in the late 1980 year by importance advances in the theory of economic growth. This period featured the development of global growth models, in which the long term rate of growth was determined within the model.

A key feature of these models is a theory of technological progress, viewed as a process whereby purposeful research and application lead over time to new and better products and methods of production by developed economic globalization. The recent growth models are useful for understanding why advanced economies and the world is as whole, can continue to grow in the long run despite the workings of diminishing returns in the accumulation of physical and human capital. These countries include, e.g. America, England which arc observed to be rich and high tend also to be those that have high long run target levels of per high capita output in a setting that includes human capital and technological change. So education is also essential to raise labour knowledge and technological level to assist developed countries, e.g. USA, UK , to raise productivity to achieve economic growth. So, the developed or developing countries' both government policies and education institutions need to concern their national population to arrange the different primary, secondary and tertiary educational policy to educate to develop whose students to develop different professional and knowledgeable and skillful abilities to already develop their careers in different nature of jobs to enter their societies to work nowadays. However, if we were the identify how education contributes to cause economic growth in any Asia developing countries. We need to compare states that have a similar distance to the frontier and yet choose difference pattern of investment in education. For example, building a new school for a research university, the process is when a vacancy arises on an committee that controls expenditure. Because governments and universities need to concern what the labour market demand, so the research university can decide prefer to choose what kinds of subjects to be taught to its potential students, e.g. medical or architect or law or engineering or business or social science, computer science etc. subjects among of them subjects, which subjects will be chosen to be taught to its potential students preferably. So, the job demand market research is very important because it can help the research university to choose what the preferable subjects will be demanded to supply to the labour market increasing in any one of Asia developing countries within future three or five years.

Theories of economic growth have emphasised the role of human capital which may affect economic growth. Human capital is as an extra input in the aggregate production function, where the output of the means economy is a direct function of factor inputs: physical capital, labor and human capital. However, technologies can raise innovate capacity of economy through developing new ideas. So, education was seemed that it could be raised graduated students' abilities to raise productivity to any one of Asia developing countries by high technological skill.

How outsourcing education strategy influences economy development to Asia countries

Any countries have two different channels through which human capital can affect long run economic growth by education provision. The first channel is when human capital is a direct input in the production function and the second channel is when the human capital affects the technology parameter. The result establishes a long run relationship between education and economic growth. A well educated labour force appears to significantly influence economic growth both as a factor in the production function and through total factor productivity. With its large resources of human and natural resources, the potential to build a prosperous economy to reduce poverty significantly and to provide the health, education services that its population needs. As the Asia developing countries, e.g. China or Korea, which are poor countries past years, which need foreign investors' different businesses development in their countries. So, themselves education is commonly regarded as the most direct avenue to rescue a substantial number of people out of poverty since there is likely to be more employment opportunities and higher wages for skilled workers. Furthermore, education can enable children's attitudes and assists them to grow up with social values that are more benefitical to their nations and themselves.

The theoretical basis of education on economic growth is rooted in the endogenous growth theory. Endogenous growth economists believe that improvements in productivity can be linked to a faster pace of innovation and extra investment in human capital. Engogenous growth theorists argue the need for government and private sector institutions and markets which need to innovate and provide incentives for individuals to be inventive. There is also a central role for knowledge as a determinant of economic growth theory can predict positive externalities and spill over effects from development of a high valued-added knowledge economy which is able to develop and maintain a competitive advantage in growth industries in the global economy.

Nowadays, education at levels countries to economic growth through imparting general attitudes and discipline and special skills necessary for a variety of work places. It contirbutes to economic growth by improving health, reducing fertility and possibly by contributing to political stability to different developing or developed both countries. The major importance of the educational system to any labor market would depend majority in ability to produce a literate, disciplines, flexible labor force via high quality education. Consequently, with economic development new technology is applied to production with results in an increase in the demand for workers and better education. In the developing countries, e.g. China, Korea, rich individuals allocate labor time not only for their own production and knowledge accumulation, but also train the poor individuals. In the past, some economists estimated a model of economic growth and human capital accumulation based on a sample of developing countries, e.g. China, Korea etc. are not a different stage of development. Their result revealed that the increase in the primary and secondary countries to an increase in productivity. They indicate that human capital acccumulation rates are affected by demographic variables. For example, they established that an increase in life expectancy at birth brings about an increase in secondary and tertiary education when a decrease in the dependence rate negatively affects secondary education. Finally, they added that geographic variables have a considerable importance in the human capital accumulation process. Nevertheless, studies differed on the impact of human capital on productivity.

The economists also indicate that human capital accumulation rates are affected by demographic variables as well as the increase in the primary and secondary level of education contibutes to an increase in productivity. For example, they established that a increase in life expectancy at birth brings about an increase in secondary and tertiary education when a decrease in the dependence rate negatively affects secondary education. However, who also believe the overall results of secondary and higher education can have a significant positive impact on growth, when primary education had not contributed to economic growth.

The GDP per unit of labor input should be related to the share of labor of a particular type (graduates or workers at different qualification levels) weighted by the average human capital of the type of worker (captured by the relative wages of different types of labor input). It seems measure of the relationship between education and productivity and economic growth can be quantified clearing to developing Asia any countries.

In past, the EUKLEMS project indicated key findings of 15 developed countries for one economic report: GDP per employment hour increased from 1992 year to 2005 year, the highest annual average percentage change was in Finland (2.7%), Japan (2.5%) and the UK (2.4%). These countries had the lowest level of GDP per employment hour in 1982 year, when the period considered the Netherlands and the USA had the highest GDP employment hour. Also it indicated the share of employment with tertiary education also increased from 1982 year to 2005 year in all countries. The highest annual average percentage change was in Australia (5%) followed by the UK (4.9%). Both of these countries had relatively low shares of employment with tertiary education in 1982 year at 6%, compared with 22.1% in the USA and 18.7% in Finland. The large increased closed the gap, but the USA and Finland still had higher employment shares with tertiary education than Australia and the UK in 2005 year. The economic report also indicatd that a 1% increase in the share of the workforce with a university degree raises the level of long run productivity by 0.2%-0.5%. So, it implied the education and productivity has close relationship to developed countries also. However, the economic benefits, both to the individual and to the wider economy of a university degree with clearly depend on the quality and skills to developing and developed countries both.

So, improvement in educational outcomes have been widely recognised as essential in enhancing growth in both developed and developing countries. In fact, education is acquire by individuals provide social returns at the macroeconomic level and addition indirect benefits to economic growth.

Firstly, I suppose it has relationship between human capital and education has close relationship to cause economic growth to any developed or developing countries both nowadays. Because if human capital and education factor has close relationship to influence any country's economic growth, then it is possible to cause productivity and economic growth has close relationship. However, some economists indicate the evidence on the relationship between human capital and economic growth and who conclude that there is strong evidence that human capital increases productivity. Suggesting that education really is productivity-enhancing, rather than education is used by individuals to signal their ability to potential employers.

The primary measures are used to capture the average level of human capital per worker include:

I. The average number of years of schooling of the

workforce or population, which assumes a linear relationship with human capital.

II. The share of the workforce population with specific educational qualifications.

III. School enrolment rates, specially as a starting value. This flow into education is often used as stock of qualifications and is available for developed Asia countries, e.g. Hong Kong, Japan and developing Asia countries, e.g. China, Korea both.

However, developing Asia countries have potential problems arising from measurement errors in education, as the average schooling levels are derived from enrolment flows. They adopt more reliable country level education micro data and find a positive result or response between the growth rate of education and economic growth. Human capital flows are most commonly provided by school enrolment rates, have been widely used in studies of the relationship between human captial and growth. This is largely due to the availability of long time series of data for a large developing or developed both Asia or foreign countries rather than because it is viewed as proferable to the human captial stock of education measures. So, based on the motivation that school enrolment rates conflate human capital stock and accumulation effects and lead to misinterpretations of the role of labor force growth. It seems education may be one of method to raise human capital and productivity growth to cause any developed or developing Asia or foreign countries‘ economic growth for long term nowadays.

Recently, the research indicates the impact of education quality is mixed. Moreover, recent studies actually suggest that education quantity is unrelated to economic growth at least in developed countries. On the other hand, a growing literature focuses on the growth impact of education quality, measures by international test scores. It finds a strong effect of education quality on economic growth when confirming that education quantity is irrelevant apart from via its impact on quality. So, I suggest the developing Asia countries' governments, e.g. China, Korea should continue their market based reforms in education. For example, by streamlining the requirements and process to establish new free schools. The goals should be to expand parental choice as widely as possible. Because education might be way to personal fulfilment, but it can also be an instrument for a healthy economy. So, reforming the education system could be a key part of any long term growth strategy to any Asia developing countries. For example, whose governments can increase spending significantly, when gradually raising the compulsory education age from 16 to 18 age following the education and skills act. Also expanding the average number of years spent in education be sufficient to improve growth. Also, any one of Asia developing countries can raise education quality more important that how much education one receives , i.e. education quantity? And how education policy can secure the highest economic dividend in as reduce efficient manner as possible. The policy implication is clear the Asia developing countries' governments should encourage an increase in the enrolment shares of independently operated schools, for example by streamlining the requirements and process to establish new free schools. A voucher system with which pupils can attend the school of their choice, either public or independent would be preferable. Such a system would sharpen competitive incentives in the education system significantly. Thus increasing the potential for choice to produce an economic dividend.

Why is education presumed to affect economic growth in any one of Asia developing countries? The main reason given is that it should improve the overall skill level, or human capital of the labor force. How human capital may be related to economic growth. Usually, capital growth is only determined by capital accumulation and technological changes. In the growth model, only technological innovation can explain long term growth because capital accumulation effects suffer from diminishing and returns. Technological change is thus the sole determinant of growth once an economy's new equilibrium/steady state (zero growth states is reached. At the same time, the sources of technological change, such as human captial are assumed to be not included as an explanatory variable in the model. In other words, the model treats education as a residual rather than as integral part of the process of change in explaining an economy's per-capita growth rate. Thus, some economists do not believe education is a conceptual tool to assist economic growth. However, some economists believe technological change and education can assist economic growth when these two factors are same to exist. Thus, education can impact growth not only by affecting innovation directly. But also by aiding the adoption of existing technology.

The augmented assumed that the effect of education eventually growth models allow education at any given level to continue to impact growth through its effect on technological change and diffusion in the economy. In other meaning, education can be provide to students to raise high technological human capital to assist economic growth. So, education can be treated as a regular factor of production to affect the growth rate in the subsequent period. This has implications for how the education variable should be included in statistical analyses, which has been a subject of debate. Otherwise, most research has focused mostly on education quantity,such as the average number of years of schooling. For example, some older studies used school enrolment rates as a measure of education. Enrolment rates impacts are being used different growth periods average over the period. It also indicates that increasing enrolment rates are positive for economic growth in developing Asia countries, e.g. China , Korea etc. In conclusion, it seems education quantity and quality as well as productivity has also relationship to influence developing Asia countries' economic growth for long term. Moreover, Asia countries choose outsourcing education which can raise students' educational level because which lack more experienced and high educational quality teachers to educate whose students. Thus, overseas teachers teach to Asia countries can give more benefits to Asia students. than Asia domestic teachers

Reference

Abrahamson, E., & Rosenkopf., (1993). Institutional and competitive bandwagons: Using mathematicalmodeling and a tool to explore innovation diffusion.

Academy of management review, 18(3), 487-517.

Hill, C.W.L. & Jones, G.R. 1995. Strategic management, An integrated approach. Boston: Houghtom Mif In.

Dimson, Marsh & Staunton, London Business School (2005) In The Global Investment Returns Year Book, ABN Amro.

Fiscal Policy And Long Term Growth, International Monetary Fund, IMF policy papers, Washington, D.C. Available from April, 2015, http://www.imf.org/external/pp/ppindex.aspx.

Kim, Y. J., and J.W. Lee 2009. Technological Change, Human Capital Structure and Multiple Growth Paths, ADB Economics Working Paper Series No. 149, Economics And Research Dept. Asian Development Bank, Manila.

CHAPTER TWO

How training brings talent employee benefit to economic development

Interview psychology methods

What are common psychology methods of recruitment choice?

Can any psychology methods are used to choose who will be the best recruitment applicant(s) in any recruitment stage more accurate? Can the interviewer observe the applicant's psychological phenomenon to judge whether the applicant can be the best or the most suitable applicant in the recruitment stage more accurate? To answer above these questions. We need to know why a systematic scientific procedure is an essential component to achieve any psychological method(s) to test candidate individual ability to judge whether who is the best or the most suitable applicant to do any position in any organization.

A psychologist can follow a systematic scientific procedure which has theoretical base in order to explain and interpret the psychological phenomenon of the applicant to decide whether who is the best or the most suitable applicant to do the position in the organization.

On the one hand, in order to obtain the applicant's psychological response from individual applicant, there are a number of psychological tools or instruments are used during the interview process. The responses are taken on these tools constitute the basic data which are analyzed to study the applicant experiences, e.g. working experiences, life experiences, mental processes and behaviors. On the other hand, in order to understand every applicant's behavior during the interview process. The different psychological methods can be applied for solving different applicant's individual behavior (individual mental problems) to judge who will be the best or the most suitable applicant to the position in any organization. Because different situations will cause the applicant to choose how to do or perform different behaviors to persuade the interviewer believes who is the best or the most suitable applicant to do the position in the organization. Thus, whose performances will be shaped by many factors both intrinsic and extrinsic to him or her in any interview process.

The common psychological methods of interview process include such as: For observation psychological method example, when shopping in the market , the researcher must have noticed various activities of the consumers . When he/she observes the consumers their activities, the researcher also think about as to why who are doing those activities and probably the researcher reaches a conclusion about the causes of such activities. So, observation is as a psychological method of enquiry is often understand as a systematic registering of events without any deliberate attempt to interface with variables operating in the event which is being studies.

Thus, observation psychological method seems to be applied to judge who is the best or the most suitable applicant to do any position in any organization in any interview process. Such as in any interview process, the interviewer (observer) can use this method to judge or observe every applicant's face and behavioral performance to feel whether who is the best or the most suitable applicant who own ability or confidence or qualification or experience to already to do the job to achieve the recruitment result is more accurate. For example, the interviewer (observer) can attempt to give one simple or difficult task to test whether whom the applicant has the more effort of the induced stress on task performance in the short time observation test in the on part stage of the interview process.

However, observation is also divided into either participant or non-participant both types, depending on the role of observer (interviewer). In the case of interview participant observation, the interviewer mixes up with the job (task) performance event test under study and conducts concerns the interview test, e.g. group discussion interview test, the applicants and the interviewer will discuss one or more than one topic(s) which concern(s) on relating the position requirement issue. So, the interviewer can analyze whom applicant(s) can talk the most reasonable evidences to support whose opinions to argue the topic against the other applicants together among of them in the short time group discussion, e.g. between 15 minutes to 30 minutes. It aims to let the interviewer can have enough time to record whose opinions to analyze whose opinions are the most reasonable argument to support whose main points to win this position among these interview competitors in the short time group discussion.

Thus, the interviewer needs to participate the group discussion to ask every applicant any questions and let them to attempt to solve any challenges in the whole group discussion. After the group discussion, then the interviewer can have more effort or confidence to judge whom applicant (s) is/are the most suitable or the best applicant (s) to do the job for his/her organization more accurate.

Otherwise, as in the case of interview non-participant observation, the interviewer maintains an optimum distance and has little impact on the interview event. Such as the interview group discussion test. The interviewer won't ask any questions to let the applicants to attempt to answer. Otherwise, he/she will let the applicants have chance to ask any questions or answer the questions among of their discussion related to the topic. So the interviewer's role is a listener, who only needs to listen every applicant how who can ask and can answer any questions to decide who can talk the most correct or the right or the most reasonable answers to answer their questions in the short time group discussion. Then, the interviewer can record all applicants' questions and answers to make the judgement to decide who will be the right or the most suitable applicant to do the position in her/him organization more accurate.

Why does need to test the applicant's psychological behavior in the interview process?

To answer this question, we need to know why any large or middle size organizations which need have human resource department. To challenge of today's HR managers is to create a pool of good employees in the organization. It starts from selection process of the employees. So, interview has been used as an important selection method by HR managers for long time. The cost of rehiring the importance of hiring the right person for right position first. It requires a reliable and valid interview process. Although, any interview won't guarantee 100 percent success in hiring the best employees into any organization, but the proper application is at least, will improve the chances of hiring the best applicant for the job the organization. The importance is given to the selection of right employees for the right positions. Firms are now realizing the value of the good employees because who can make a difference through their job performance. So, various selection methods are now being used to identify the right candidate.

" Interview" has emerged as a very useful tool in this regard. It is a very common selection method and has a high predictive validity for job performance (Robertson, & Smith , 2001). The main purpose of the interview is to select the right candidate for the right job. The importance of conducting an effective interview is also rising. So consensus was found among the HR experts regarding the effective interview techniques. There are a number of existing literatures regarding the techniques of an effective interview, but every few literatures exist regarding a systematic approach of conducting exist regarding a systematic approach of conducting an effective interview.

This is a very few literatures exist regarding a complete interview process that shows a clear path to the employers for selecting right employees. A lot of interview technique are available, but the problem arises regarding the use of these techniques in a concrete manner. A systematic approach of interview will facilitate the tasks of HR managers in selecting the right applicant for the right position.

(Stevens, 1997) author indicated the whole process of the interview has been described in terms of "3D"- Development, discussion and decision. This study is particularly important for three reasons. First , it will help the HR mangers to think about the employee selection interview in a concrete manner. Second, it will help them to use a number of interview techniques in an effective way that will ultimately increase the chance of hiring the right person for the right position. Third, it will enrich the existing literature of selection interview.

(Stevens, 1997) author also explained that the growing importance of good employees will cause a challenge to the HR managers. The selection process of today's HR manager is becoming complex and challenging. Undoubtedly, the overall aim, of the selection process is to identify the candidates who are suitable for the vacancy or wider requirement of the HR plan. " Interview" has been used as a ' critical selection method ' by HR managers. The interview is the most valid method in determining an applicant's organizational fit, level of motivation and inter-personal selects.

Whetton & Cameron (2002) cited steps of process of conducting an interview, what they named as People-oriented selection interview process. Here is explains the interview process: P=prepare, E=establish rapport, O=obtain information, P=provide information, C= lead top close and E= evaluate.

So, it seems that the candidates' behavior individual performance in the interview process can be predicted whether who is(are) the most suitable or the best to do the position in the organization from the interviewer's observation. So, it also means the candidate's attitude in the interview process can perform to let the interviewer to feel whether who is suitable or the best to do the position in the organization . Thus, observation of the applicant individual performance, it is an interviewer's best interest to find good prospects, hire them and have them stay in the organization.

Therefore, the interviewees are needed to be provided sufficient information about the job and organization to have enough time to prepare before who will go to interview fairly. It aims to let every candidate has enough confidence to prepare to answer any questions in further interview process fairly. So, the development stage is a good preparation for the interview facilitates the effective interview process. To aim to let the candidate have enough preparation to interview , it should begin long before the first question is ever asked fairly.

In conclude, HR department seems an essential department to any middle or large organizations nowadays. It does not attribute only recruitment function to any organization, it also attribute the chance to give one psychological test function to evaluate whom applicant has the more experience and qualification and effort to do any position in any organization. If the interviewer has not prepared any psychological method to test any applicants to judge whether who has the more effort to do the position. Then, I believe the interview result will be more failure and more inaccurate to employ the most suitable applicant , due to who lacks the enough effort and qualification and experience to perform to finish any tasks or duties of the position . So, it is important why any organization needs have good psychological method to test and observe the applicant's psychological behavior in the interview process?

Occupation psychological test methods

How to apply psychological recruitment strategies effect/manage in the recruitment process?

HR (human resource) managers understand accept that poor recruitment decisions continue to affect organizational performance and limit goal achievement. In this case, many jurisdictions to identify and implement new effective hiring strategies will be serious issue to any HR departments to concern.

Acquiring and retaining high-quality talent is critical to any organization's success. So, recruiters need to be more elective in their choice. Since poor recruiting decisions can produce long term negative effects, among their high training and development costs to minimise the incidence of poor performance and high turnover to impact staff morale, the production of high quality goods and services. Thus, HR managers must seek all possible methods for improve their output and provide the satisfaction to their clients require and deserve. The provision of high quality goods and services begins with the recruitment process.

(Schuler, Randalls, 1989) explained recruitment is as " the set of activities and processes used to legally obtain a sufficient number of qualified applicants at the right place and time. So that the applicants and the organization can select each other in their own best short and long term interests.

Thus, it seems that successful recuritment begins with proper employment planning and forecasting. So any one organization needs analyze what kinds of positions of future needs talent available within and outside of the organization and the current and anticipated resources that can be expected to attract and retain such talent. Thus, HR manager needs have one successful strategy to be prepared to employ in order to identify and select the best candidates for its developing pool of human resources.

In common, one successful recuruitment strategy involves these several processes of :

Step one : Development of a policy on recruitment and giving life to the policy.

Step two: Needing assessment to determine the current and future human resource requirement of the organization.

Step three: If the activity is to be effective , the HR requirements for each job category and functional division /unit of the organization must be assessed, identification within and outside the organization of the potential human resources pool.

Step four: Job analysis and job evaluation to identify the individual aspects of each jobs and calculate its relative worth, assessment of qualifications profiles, job descriptions that identify responsibilities and requirement skills, abilities , knowledge and experience, determination to pay salaries and benefits within a defined period.

Step five: identification and documentation of the actual process of recruitment and selection to ensure equity and laws.

Thus, the psychological recruitment strategy for the interviewer includes how to ask interview questions, how to give interview scores and panellists' comments, results of tests (where administered). Because and length of interview time for the interview. There are any interview main contents to any interviewer needs to concern how to arrange interview process.

For example, nowadays, it is popular internet recruiting. Although, interviewer can reduce time to arrange and spend time to interview any applicants, due to the interviewer can interview any applicants from whose organization website . Specially, there are many similar potential interview competitors to apply to the position at the same time. Otherwise, internet recruiting is not all positive. Such as some applicants skill place great value in face-to-face interactons in the hiring process. Such applicant;s are likely to ignre jobs posted, impersonally on time.

I shall indicate these sample recruitment strategy to explain how to influence every applicant's choice to apply the job or not apply the job as below:

The first is online recruiting. This online recuritment strategy has a large percentage of employees are hired by human service agencies for every level jobs are seeking their first career job. The newspaper want ads are not an effective recruitment source for most of today's applicants. Placing vacancy announcements online is more effective and economical than using most traditional forms of advertising. However, online recruitment is designed to close this gap: Not reaching majority of applicants, especially young graduates.

The second is campus recruiting and job fairs. This campus recruiting strategy attracts both professional and paraprofessional applicants, who can be effectively recruited at job fairs sponsored by state workforce development agencies. However, college recruiting can be a very effective method for attracting applicants for professional jobs. The possible psychological advantages to applicants that includes any employers will send team of HR representatives to any colleges to provide an opportunity for job seekers to ask both job specific and hiring process/benefits questions; sending an ambassador to classrooms to quest lecture; schedule experienced employees or supervisors to ask on a hot topic in the human or service field at a local college or university. However, this campus recruiting strategy has a large percentage of employees hired, but need to improve overall applicant.

The third is university partner developing a variety of recruitment strategy. University partnership benefits include to collaborate with university deans and professors to help student interest in the field as well as to develop program partially covering college tuition and other expenses of college students who agree to work for the human service agency for specified periods of time. Its recruitment strategy aims to develop a variety of recruitment strategies with area universities, community colleges and schools of social work to encourage students to pursue careers in the human services. It's weakness lacks enough applicants with specialized social work degrees.

The fourth recruitment strategy is target recruitment. Employers may used a more diverse workforce that better reflects the client population who serve. For example, employers may need to recruit employees with specific lannguage skills or with specialized degrees , e.g. criminal juice. It' weakness lacks of diversity in targeted jobs.

The fifth recruitment strategy is internships. Interns sometimes are paid stipend, but in most instances interns are fulfilling an academic requirement of the college or university. Although supervisors and/or cause work staff must spend time supervising and training interns, the potential payoff is having a known applicant who is familiar with agency operations. Its weakness is needed to improve overall applicant pool.

The sixth recruitment strategy is maintain a pre-screened applicant pool. It has a pool of pre-screened, interviewed applicants always available to be called for a second interview with the hiring supervisor. When, using this approach, it's important to minimize the amount of time between the initial interview and the second interview to prevent top quality applicants from being hired human resources will need to do continuous recruiting and screening , even when there are no current vacancies. It's weaknesses include that some
human services organizations delay hiring until staff vacancies reach crisis proportions. They than initiate a recruitment process that is designed to bring new employees on board as soon as possible . The unfortunate result is hiring employees who meet the minimum requirements, but nothing more. It also has too many applicants get hired with only the minimum credentials.

The seventh recruitment strategy is realistic job previews. Realistic job previews are designed to prevent applicants from taking jobs that who have life knowledge of or are not suited to perform. It is a recruiting tool is designed to reduce early turnover by communicating both the desirable and the undesirable aspects of a jobs before applicants accept a job offer. It can be in the form of videos, oral presentations, job shadowing opportunities. It's weakness includes unwanted turnover among new workers who did not understand their job when who were hired.

The final recruitment strategy is improved hiring flexibilities in highly centralized systems. It means many public-seator human service agencies are regulated by merit systems that make it different to attract and maintain the interest of top-qualify applicants. Top applicants in today's economy are searching the interest for jobs that are available now. They aren't interested in taking a civil service exam and sitting on eligibility lists for months. In some systems requirements and lengthy inflexible scoring processes wash out well qualified applicants. It's weaknesses include hiring process takes too long, high qualify applicants are looking elsewhere for jobs.

How to apply occupational psychological test method to test applicant's ability?

Occupational psychological interview method is the application of the science of psychology to test applicant individual work ability. For example, any interviews can apply occupational psychologists' test method to attempt to test applicant individual performance, motivation and wellbing of the organization in the workplace. If any interviewers can attempt to apply occupational psychologist test method to test any applicant individual working abilities in interview. It brings this question: How can the interviewer develop, apply and evaluate a range of tools and interventions to test the applicant individual working abilities across many different areas of the workplace?

The occupational psychological test method can include these psychological skills to test every applicant individual ability in interview. Such as : Psychological assessment means selecting and assessing the applicant individual ability using interview enquiring method, e.g. in interview, enquiring applicant concerns on how to solve crisis deal issues when challenges cause in any workplace, assessments of what the applicant's main ability centres are. Situational judgement tests, e.g. how to solve challenges in different situations and personality questionnaires and cognitive ability tests. Profiling jobs are matching requirements to the applicant's future performance. Developing and choosing is valid, reliable, fair and suitable selectin procedures.

Thus, the psychological enquiring questions can concern on work motivation, performance, appraisal and management, leadership power influence and negotiation, employee engagement and commitment, citizenship and positive behaviors or counterproductive in workplace, psychology of group teams and teamwork different aspects, which have similar points , such as concern organizational behavior questions. It aims to test the applicant how to deal any immediate crisis in the organization if the interviewer decides to employ him/her.

The key focus of how to achieve one effective psychological test to the applicant in the interiew. It focuses on key areas , such as the applicant personal goal attainment, interview performance, the applicnt's mind on innovation and creativity aspects, and well being in the workplace how the applicant explains who will perform supposes who did the job in the workplace.

In the interview, the interviewer needs the applicant to explain to let him/her to understand how the applicant's relation and motivation in the organization. The interviewer also needs to know how the applicant can solve any challenges in workplace in the suitation test interview. Because conflict resolution is a challenging environment to work in. However, any downsides are offset by the rewards of being able to help protect both the organization and its employees from the psychological , physiological and economic costs of conflict. Because conflict will occur in possible in any workplaces. Thus, the interviewer ought to ask the question to let him/her to know the applicant will solve if who did this position.

Human factors is a discipline concerned with how the successful interview applicant (future employee) works effectively and safely. It considers a employee's environmental , organizational, job and individual characteristics. These factors will affect the organizational successful interview applicant (future employee) behavior and it is past of the interviewer's job to analyze these and to give recommendations for change to improve human performance to the organization if who selected to employ these applicants in every time interview. Thus it seems occupational psychological test method can give benefits to the interviewer to understand more to the applicants to judge whether who will be the most suitable applicant(s)to do any positions in whose organization more accurate decision in any interviews.

Selecting and evaluating assessment methods

How selection assessment methods are applied to choose the best applicants ?

Organizations compete in the war for talent. So, one effective selection assessment method can help any organizations to choose the best applicant(s). Using scientifically proven assessments to make selection decisions, even though such assessments have been shown to result in significant productivity increases, cost savings, decrease other critical organizational outcomes. I shall indicate common misconceptions about selection tests, such as: Screening applicants for conscientiousness will yield better performers , then screening applicants for intelligence, screening applicants for their values will yield better performers , then screening applicants for intelligence, integrity tests are not ueful because job candidates misrepresent themselves on these typs of tests, unstructured interviews with candidates provide better information than structured assessment processes and using selection tests creates legal problems for organizations rather than helps to solve them.

There are numerous different types of formal assessments that organizations can use to select employees. The first step in developing or selecting an assessment method for a given situation is to understand what the job requires employees to do and what knowledge, skills and abilities individuals must posses in order to perform the job effectively. This is typically accomplished by conducting a job analysis . For job oriented job analysis recruitment example, providing test by stating fact and answer questions, gathering and reviewing information to obtain obtain evidence or develop background information on subjects, integrating diverse information to uncover relationships between individuals, events or evidences.

Other assessment methods focus on how measuring the best applicant who are required to perform job tasks effectively, such as various mental abilities, physical abilities or personality traits, depending on the job's requirements. If one were to assess whether candidates could solve decisive and communicate effectively. Alternatively, if one were selecting an administrative assistant, such as the ability to perform work conscientiously with speed and accuracy would be such more important for identifying capable candidates. Some worker-oriented or job analysis data are used as a basis for developing assessment method, that focus on a job candidate's underlying abilities to perform important work task.

In general, any organization interviews only divide either internal or external both selection. Internal selection refers to situations where organization is hiring or promoting from within, whereas, external selection refers to situations where an organization is hiring from the outside. When some assessent methods are used more commonly for external selection. (e.g. cognitive ability tests, personality tests, integrity tests). There are numerous examples of organizations that have used one or more of the following tools for internal selection, external selection or both. I shall explain what the differences for these interview test methods as follow:

What is cognitive ability tests. These assessment measure a variety of mental abilities, such as verbal and mathematical ability, reasoning ability and reading comprehension. Cognitive ability tests have been shown to be extremely useful predictors of job performance and thus are used frequently in making selection decisions for many different types of jobs (Hunter, J. 1986, Ree, M.J. & Teachout, M.S. 1984, Gottredson, L.S. 1982).

Cognitive ability tests typically consist of multipler choice items that are administered via a paper-and-pencil instructment or computer. Some cognitive ability tests contain test items that need various abilities, e.g. verbal ability, numberical ability etc. But then sum up the correct answers to all of the items to obtain a singl total score. The total score then represents a measure of general mental ability. If a separate score is computed for each of the specific types of abilities, then the resulting scores represent measures of the specific mental abilities.

Job knowledge tests mean these assessments measure critical knowledge areas that are needed to perform a job effectively. Typically, the knowledg areas measured represent technical knowledge. Job knowledge tests are used in situations m where candidates must clearly possess a body of knowledge prior to job entry. Job knowledge tests are not appropriate to use in situations where candidates will be trained after selection on the on knowledge areas who need to have. Like cognitive ability tests, job knowledge tests typically consist of multiple-choice items administered via a paper-and-pencil instrument or a computer , although essay items are sometimes included in job knowledg tests (Hunter, J. 1986).

Personality tests that assess traits relevant to job performance have been shown to be effective predictors of subsequent job performance. The personality factors that are assessed most frequently in work situations include conscientiousness, extraversion, agreeableness, openness to experience and emotional stability (Barrick, M.R. & Mount, M.K. 1991, Costa, P.T. Jr., & Mccae, r. R. 1982).

Research has shown that conscientiousness is the most useful predictor of performance across many different jobs. Although some of the other pesonality factors have been shown to be useful predictors of peformance in specific types of jobs (Hough, L.M. 1992). It can consist of several multipe choice or true/false items measuring each personality factor. Like cognitive ability and knowledge tests, which are also administered in a paper-and-pencil or computer format.

Biographical data (biodata) inventories, which ask job candidates questions covering their background, personal characteristics or interests have been shown to be effective predictors of job performance (Stokes, G.S. & Owens, W.A. 1994, Shoenfeldt, L.F. 1999). Another form of a biodata inventory is an instrument called an " accomplishment stored". With this types of assessment, candidates prepare a written account of their most meritorious accomplishments in key skill and ability areas that are required for a job , e.g. planning and organizing, customer service, conflict resolution (Hough, L.M. 1984).

Integrity tests measure attitudes and experiences that are related to an individual honesty, trustworthiness and dependability (Sackett, P.R. & Wanek, J.E. 1996). It is typically multiple-choice in format and administered via a paper-and-pencil instrument or a computer.

Physical fitness tests are used in some selection situations. These tests require candidates to perform general physical activities to assess one's overall fitness, strength or other physical capabilities necessary to perform the job.

Situational judgement tests provide job candidates with situations that who would encounter on the job and viable options for handling the presented situations (Mecichmann, D., Schmitt, N. & Harvey, V.S. 2001). depending on how the test is designed , candidates are asked to select the most effective or most and least effective ways of handling the situaton from the response options provided. Situational judgement tests are more complicated to develop than many of the other types of assessments. It is because more difficulty in developing scenarios with several likely response options that are all viable, but in fact, some are reliably rated as being more effective than others. Situational judgement tests are typically administered in written or paper-and-pencil test booklet or on a computer.

Assessment centers are a type of work sample test that is typically focused on assessing higher-level managerial and supervisory competencies (Thornton, G.C III 1992). Assessment centers usually last at least a day and up to several days. They typically include role-play exercises in -basket exercises, analytical exercises and group discussion exercises. Trained assessors observe the performane of candidates during the assessment process and evaluate them on standardized rating. Some assessment centers also include other types of assessment methods, such as cognitive ability, job knowledge and personality tests. It should be noted selection purposes that assessment centers aren't only used for comprehensive development feedback to participants.

Physical ability tests are used regularly to select workers for physiclly demanding jobs, such as police officers and firefighters. These test are similar to work sample tests in that who typically require candidates to perform a series of actual job tasks to determine whether or not who can perform the physical requirements of a jobs. Physical ability tests are often scored in a pass/fail basis. To pass, the complete set of taks that comprise the test must be properly completed within a specified timeframe.

How to criteria for selecting and evaluating assessment methods in interview?

Properly identifying and implementing formed assessment methods to select employees is one of the more complex areas for HR department to learn about and understand. This is because understanding selection testing requires knowledge of statistics, measurement issues and legal issues relevant to testing.

I recommend any interviewers need to understand important criteria to decide to choose which kind of interview test is the suitable to test applicant individual abilities in every interview such as below:

The first criteria includes validity. Validity means the extent to which the assessment method is useful for predicting subsequent job performance. Adverse impact means the extent to which protected group members , e.g. minorities, females and individualds over 40 score lower on the assessment than majority group members.

The second criteria includes cost. Cost is both to develop and to administer the assessment. Applicant reactions means the extent to which applicants react positively versus negtively to the assessment method. For example, cognitive ability test. on the positive side, this type of assessment is high on validity and low on costs. However, it is also high on adverse impact, moderately favorable. Thus, when cognitive tests are inexpensive and very useful for predicting subsequent job performance, minoritie score significantly lower on them than whites. There is no simple, formulaic approach for selecting " one best" assessment method, because all of them have advantages and disadvantages.

However, the most important consideration in evaluating on assessment method is its validity. Validity refers to whether or not the assessment method provides useful information about how effectively an employee will actually perform once who is hired for a job. Validity is the most important factor in considerating whether or not to use an assessment method because identify who will doesn't accurately identify who will perform effectively on a job has no value to the organization.

There are two major forms of validity: criterion-related validity and content validity is a simple example will illustrate how criterion-related validity can be established. Assume that a sales job requires employees to have a high level of customer service orientation and an organization decides to implement a selection test that assesses prospective applicants on their customer service skills. In order to show that the client skills assessment is a valid predictor of peformance , it must be shown that individuals who score higher on the assessment perform better. On the job and individuals who score lower on the assessment perform less well on the job. Thus, validity in this case would be defined as a meaningful relationship between how well people performed on the assessment and how well who subsequently performed on the job. Content validity approach to validation involves demonstrating that an assessment provides a direct measure of how well candidates will actually perform to job. This type of validation requires analyzing the job to identify the tasks that are performed.

What are the differences between criterion related versus content validation. Criterion-related validity can be used to evaluate the validity of any assessment where individuals receive scores that reflect how well who perform on the test and these scores are subsequently shown to relate to how well who perform on the job. Content validation can only be used to validate assessments that provide a direct measure of how well candidates perform job tasks or the content of the jobs, such as work sample tests. Otherwise, criterion-related validity evidence or contect validity . Thus, it is more desirable to obtain if it is possible to conduct a successful unbiased performance measures must be available. Unfortunately, performance appraisal ratings, which are the most commonly used performance measures can be inaccurate and often fail.

Adverse impact is examined by comparing the proportion of majority group who are selected from a job to the protected group members who are selected. When organizations are and should be interested in selecting the higher quality work force possible, many are also concerned about selecting a diverse workforce ought not using measures that will systematically produce adverse impact against protected groups.

In conclusion, either if an assessment method is shown to produce adverse impact and the organization wished to continue the last of that assessment, there are legal requirements to ensure that the method must have demonstrated validity or if an organization uses an assessment that produces adverse impact that produces adverse impact without the validity evidence. The organization will encounter challenges against which it won't be able to prevail. When evidence of validity can be used to justify and defend the use of measures that produce an adverse impact many organizations nonetheless attempt to apply the adverse impact produced be their assessment methods to extent possible in order to minimize potential interview wrong recuritment decisions and lack of diversity concerns issues to recruit any the most suitable applicants to do any positions in any organizations.

Reference

Barrick, M. R. & Mount , M.K. (1991). The big five personality dimensions and job performance: A meta-analysis, personnel psychology, 91, 1-26.

Costa, P.T. & Jr., & McCrae, R.R. (1992). Four ways five factors are basic. Personality and individual differences, 13,

653-665.

Gottredson, L.S. (Ed). (1982). The g factor in employment, Journal of vacational behavior, 29(3).

Hough, L.. (1992) The big five personality variables construct confusion: Description versus prediction human performance, 5, 135-155.

Hough, L.M. (1984). Development and evaluation of the " accomplishment record" methods of selecting and promoting professonals. Journal of applied psychology, 69, 135-146.

Hunter, J. (1986). Cognitive ability, cognitive aptitudes, job knowledge and job performance, Journal of vacational behavior, 29, 340-362.

Meichmann, D., Schmitt, N., & Harvey, V.S. (20010. Incremental validity of situatinal judgement tests , Journal of applied psychology, 86, 410-417.

Ree, M.J. Earles, J.A., & Teachout, M.S. (1994), Predicting job performance: Hot much more than g. Journal of applied psychology, 79, 518-524.

Robserton, I. T., & Smith, M. (2001). Personnel Selection. Journal Of Occupational And Organizational Psychological Psychology, 74(4), 441-472.

Sackett, P.R. & Wanek, J.E. (1996). New developments in the use of measures of honesty, integrity, conscientiousness, dependability, trustworthiness and reliability for personnel selection, personnel psychology, 49, 787-829.

Schuler, Randalls, S: Personnel and human resources management. Third edition, 1987.

Shoenfeldt, L.F. (1999). From dustbowl empiricism to rational constructs in biodata. Human resource management review, 9, 147-167.

Steven, Kay Cynthia (1997). Effects of pre-interview beliefs on applicant's reactions to campus interviews. Academy of management journal, 40(4), 947-966.

Stokes, G.S. Mumford, M.D. & owen, W.A. (Eds.) (1994). Biodata handbook paloacto, CA: CPP Books.

Thornton, G.C. III (1992). Assessment centers in human resources management Addison-Wesley,

Whetton, D.A. & Cameron, K.S. (2002). Developing Management , Skill 5th edition, reading, MA: Addison Wesley Longman.

Developing a successful employee training program steps

To develop one successful employee training program, any employer must need to follow these steps to achieve to train employees to raise efficiencies and improving performance successfully. I recommend these steps to develop one successful training program as below:

The first step: Calculation to every training budget, its needs how much costs to implement. Because designing and arranging one successful training program. It needs expenditure to buy the training course materials, tutors employment and rent office or hotel hall to teach the organizational employees expenditure.

However, training has been proven an important part of continued growth and forward movement for both the employee and the organization as a whole. The organization needs to spend too much money and time to organize any training department programs justified and ensure return on investment. Hence, expenditure budget is needed to evaluate how to spend how much on trainers employment expenditure, courses teaching purchase expenditure, rent office or hotel hall for training teaching expenditure. For example, if the training program needs to spend long time to teach or train employees. It will cause too much training expenditure is needed for long time training period.

So, an absolute training program expenditure budget, e.g. every month, every quarter, every half year, even every year training program budget expenditure. It can avoid actual training expenditure which will exceed budget training expenditure for long time in order to organization's training department.

The second step: Deciding what type of training is needed? Training should be provided before problems or accidents occur. This step is to identify what is needed for people to do their jobs in a safe and productive way. New recruits may need basic training where more experienced workers only need refresher training. To avoid unnecessary training, it is equally important to determine wht kind of training, it is equally important to determine what kind of training is not needed.

The third step: Identifying goals and objectives for your every training program. Clearly stated goals and objectives will identify what your employer to do, to do better, or to stop doing. They don't necessarily have to be written, but in order for the training to be successful, objectives should be thought out before the training begins. Such as when should the training occur? Is it initial training or refresher? Will training include hands-on use of equipment? How much time will be required to training? How will training affect production? Will training be scheduled during work hours or using overtime?

So, when you ensure whether what goals or objectives are for you training program. Then, you will analyze whether you organization is really needed one training program to train your employees or not.

The fourth step: Conducting the training program. Training conducted is needed by professionals will knowledge and expertise in the given subject area is most successful. There are many different methods available to training. It should allow employees to participate in the training process and to practice their skills or knowledge.

The fifth step:Evaluating the effectiveness, testing and evaluating is necessary to measure the success of training. Testing at the ned of training helps determine the amount of learning achieved. providing a training evaluation worksheet following the training program will measure the comfort level and understanding of the training they received. The trainees will also tell the trainers if they feel the trainers are qualified. Also, employees should immediately use the skills they know.

How supervisors observe new and transfer employees to determine of they are doing the job right and they are using the new skills. If the employees don't understand the information they learned in training, they will not use it.

The sixth step: Improving the training program, if after evaluation, it is clear that the necessary to revise the training program. Employers need to ensure every employee has been given the necessary information and training that will enable them to perform their job duties safely. In addition, you might using a different method or facilitator. Asking questions of employees, other training peers and of those who conducted the training may be of some help in improving any of the organization's training programs.

The final step: Designing the suitable type of training. How to design the suitable type of training program, it is very important to train every trainee to achieve their learning aim effectively. The types of training program may

include as below:
(1) On -the -job training by peers or group training by management. It's advantages include that questions are easily answered based on experience, trainees are production with less cost and time since training is on-the-job. Trainees hear the same thing from peers working in field. Usually, there is more training time since it is continue.
However it's disadvantges include that trainees learn habits that might be unsafe, there is less control over what traninee's learn, trainees require a good trainer to ensure information is communicated properly and trainees may be rushed and not get adequate training if time is limited. It will influence whose job performance if they can't get adequate training, but they need to do their jobs as the same time.

(2) Next is live instructor lead training by a outside professional. It's advantages include trainees are motivated to learn because of personal attention by outside trainer, the weaknesses or wrong vire points easily identified by professional and are corrected at the time of training, training content is more controlled and objective, job interruptions are limited. So, trainees can focus on training only.
However, it has also disadvantages include that the organization may require a good trainer. He/she may be ill-prepared or unfamiliar with your organization. It could be more costly. The live outside instructor may be difficult to coordinate with other departments and arrangement. The class schedue may be difficult.

(3) Finally, it is electronic instruction on video based/ computer assisted training program. It's advantages include that the trainer doesn't need to go to school classroom

or workplace or hotel hall or company training room to teach his/ner trainees. He/she can be self directed or self controlled time from video face-to-face computer training channel contact. It is good for annual or refreshed training, virtual environment may be favorable to production , it can be cost effective, due to not need to pay too much prebooking school classrooms or hotel halls rent for training many employee number every time, e.g. 100 to 1000 trainee number.

In conclusion, all above steps are essential needed to follow to arrange for every training program to any organization. So, trainer must not neglect all any one of these steps if the trainer hope whose training program can be achieved to raise every employee performance and efficiency after they attend the training program.

- What kinds of organizations need training program

I believe innovative organizations need training program to assist whose organizations internal department. What is training and development mean? It means a function of human resource management and it concerns with organizational activity aimed at improving the performance of individuals and groups in organizational strategies. It has been known by human resource development and learning and development.

Why does innovative organization need training program? When an organization is felt that it needs to be innovated, then training and development will be also needed. Training and development is a subsystem of an organization. It ensures that unnecessary repeated or inefficient or unmeaning jobs are reduced and learning or behavioral change takes place in structured format.

So, training and development or learning and development

is one of the most important organizations which have better performance or efficiency change to be designed to enhance the fulfillment and performance of employees. So, it brings training and development programs are needed to be offered by a innovative organization might include a variety or educational techniques and programs that can be attened on a compulsory or voluntary basis by staff.

Before any organization's innovation, in general, they never used to believe in training. They were holding the traditional view that managers have responsibilities and effort to do training activities and training is a very costly affair and not worth. But, now the scenario seems to be changed. The modern approach of training and development is that organizations have realized the importance of corporate training. The training industry has been changed to create a smarter workforce and active the best performance improvement and raising efficiency result.

Training and development includes three activities: training, education and development. Training is one activity is both focused upon, and evaluate against, the job that an individual currently holds.

(1) Education is one activity foucuses upon the jobs that an individual may potentially hold in the future, and is evaluated against these jobs.

(2) Development is one activity, focuses upon the activities the organization employing the individual, or that the individual is part of may partake in the future and is almost impossible to evaluate in long term plan.

When an organization is innovated by achieving training program. It will earn these benefits as below:

(1) Discovering or finding employee weaknesses: Most workers have certain weaknesses in their workplace.

Training assists in eliminating those weaknesses by strengthening workers skills. A well organized development program helps employees gain similar skills and knowledge ,thus bringing them all to a higher uniform level. It is simply that the whole workforce is reliable, so the whole company or one department doesn't have to rely only on specific employees.

(2) Improvement in workers performance: It is a properly trained employees become more informed about procedures for various tasks needs. The workers confidence is also boostes by training and development. This intangible confidence effort comes from the fact that the employee is fully aeare of his/her role and responsibilities. It helps the worker carry out the duties in better way.

(3) Consistency in duty performance a innovated organization gives the constant knowledge and experience. Consistency is very important when it cases to an change organization's procedures and policies and ethics during execution of duty to all different level of employees from top to down levels.

(4) Raising worker satisfaction: Training and development can drive the great ability to let employees to feel they belong to the company or the organization that they require for and the only way to reward, it is giving the best services they can after they attend any training programs to let they know, and they can judge whether their job degre and effort can achieve to satisfy their organization's demand.

(5) Raising employee individual productivity and improving quality of services: Employees can acquire all the knowledge any one of training program. When they can not learn or feel tasks. Workers can perform at a faster rate and with efficiency thus increasing overall productivity of

the company as well as they also gain new duties of overcoming challenges when they face them.

Also, employees can gain standard methods to use in their tasks to maintain uniformity in the output they give. Even reduced cost in supervision, training and development can utilize resources and there is no wastage of resources reducing extra expenses which can caused by accidents occurrence changes during they are working.

Thus, considerately the expected innovative organizations ought choose to set up one training and development department to train trainers to teach trainees in order to raise whose efficiencies and improve performance for whole efficiencies and improve performance for whole organization's innovation aim achievement.

- Reasons of employee training fails and how to solve

In fact, if organizations can not apply corrective ways to facilitate training for employees. It won't improve engagement, productivity and staff retention effectively. The question is why training program can not guarantee any organizations to achieve performance improvement and efficiencies.

The reason is simply. Because these fail training organizations apply wrong training methods, so they can not achieve to improve efficiency and performance under the least budget expenditure spending. The reasons include as below:

(1) The traditional training method is not suitable or still effective to the organization, e.g. it can not help the organization to improve skills, boost morale and build good teams and work processes. I recommend that to maximum the impact of training investment. Organization leader needs to understand how to choose the right training programs, when they need to arrange training and how to

select training for the future.

Training must be satisfied to the needs of the organization's staff. The perfect training program ought be excited, interest and engaged the trainees, which encourages them to make use of the training when they need to do their day-to-day jobs to deliver the right training is so important to trainees.

(2) The boring training presentation. Another reason is possible that the trainees feel the training program is bored. It is simply repeat what is being said by the presenter. The audiences feel all the training courses are similar and they are very attractive. So, the training presenter ought consider training time is precious time and organization is paying it, he/she ought not waste organization's precious time to attempt to train whose audiences. So, choosing the right training, it is the trainer's responsibility and he/she must sure that time and money is spent effectively and the organization must get the best return.

So, choosing what kinds of training fastor which is important to influence whether the training is successful or fail. The different kinds of training may include: 3 D virtual learning and video tuition, face-to-face training, self and paced learning and webiners , e-learning and social learning. For example, e-learning is becoming more popular organizations realize the potential of training staff at their own time and with the least impact to productivity. It is one kind of skillsoft offer, a wide range of stimulating, engaging and effective learning option. It is different to traditional face-to-dce training. It is exciting, fun internet training tool to let every trainee to talk between them and trainer to discuss any training topic and it can let the trainer explains to them to let they listen and see them clearly by e-learning video tool at home conveniently.

The another training fail reason is that it is important to arrange training that repects that every trainee has different learning styles and rates. Not every trainee is going to want to lead a discussion or be led. A good training course is one that allows everybody to get involved through a range of different methods.

In response to these requirements, skill-soft offers a range of memorable and engaging video-based presentations is the best training to listen the trainer's presentation only, when he/she is watching the video. So, they do not need to discuss and the trainer doesn't need to lead them to listen every online training program. When the trainer arrange the date and time to let all trainees to turn on computer. Then, they can watch the trainer's face and listen whose presentation from onlin video attentively. The trainees will be attractive from the trainer's online training presentation.

This online training method is more better than traditional classroom or workplace training course because a boring class is often the sign of a training provider who has not put enough effort into winning trainees' attention. However, e-learning techniques give mployees access to wider range of trining resources than ever before . They can watch videos, interact with others on the same course and revise topcis at their leisure.

Finally, the training fail reason is that without good planning to a new training program. So, I recommend any one expected training organization nees to consider these factors are related to how to plan good training such as below:

What skills and competencies are required across the training preparation?

Are these skills gaps across the organization?

How to solve these softskills gaps before to achieve one training?

Has the organization developed a training strategy that will ensure training is invested in with the objectives of the company in mind?

Has the organization developed an similar training implementation plan?

How and when will training be delivered?

Can it deliver this training program efficiently, attractively, satisfactory to rais employee productivity efficiencies and improve performance absolutely?

Consequently, I recommend whole organization's top to down level employees who need to participate how to prepare the new training program planning in order to avoid its failure chance. The top level includes executive and senior level managers, the middle level includes middle managers and supervisors and the low level includes the trainers ot the training program. Because training course preparation is whole organization management duty. It is ont only training deparment duty. So, above all these staffs must need to consider how to plan to achieve the training program successfully.

● Prediction rewards and costs of training program

How to calculate every different kinds of training rewards and costs? How to evaluate the training whether it is worth to spend time and time to invest to train employees (trainees)? Whether does the organization need to arrange one training program to let employees (trainees) to be learn new skill knowledge? To answer these question: I shall assume one training program is such as one lotteruy, the lottery buyer will not know whether he/she will win ot lose the lottery, but he/she does not attempt to buy the lottery who won't have chance to win the lucky money.

So, one training program is such one lottery. Whether at the organization as part of a training department of the organization, the training time and money and teaching course material and trainers and training teaching method etc. arrangement must be dominated by the trainer and organization's time. It is determined by their moods. These factors will influence whether the training program can receive rewards or not after it is spent any expenditures are related to the training. Hence, the organization must not know whether how much rewards will be caused by the training program. It only know to plan how much expenditure budget will be spent to the training program. So, training seems to be one lottery game to be played by the player, he/she needs to spend money and time to participate the lottery game.

Training course is similar to lottery game, the organization needs to spend time and money to arrange trainer and trainees to participate the training program. Hence, whether the worth of training which can earn rewards or not, it needs time to wait. It is hard to predict training reward.

Indeed, economists tend to be unexpectedly indifferent to matters of money, such as cost of every training program. It is a complicating superficial distraction that can usually be assumed away without much harm being (trainer and trainees, employees) done, such as waste or loss of the organization's time and money and human resource to prepare every training program.

It may be natural to look to economics for guidance about earnings, such as future every training program reward. However, when any organization expects to innovate its working environment, office politics, increasing truth, employee royalty, honestry and lies avoidance, raising every high management, middle management and low level working employee individual power and fair promotion, which must need to accept to choose to arrange any suitable training program to satisfy every high management, middle managers and low worker level skills and psychological needs in order to raise their efficiency and productivity and performance effectively. Hence, every organization's innovation aim is similar to playing one lottery game. When the organization can achieve its innovation intention or aim after every different kind of training program.

Then, if it can innovate all its policy, strategy, improving every employee work efficiency and performance, raising productivity etc. different aspects successfully. I believe the organization must earn more reward, due to it has one successful innovation after every different of training to be provided to satisfy all different levels of employee needs from top to low level in the organization.

One open organization is applied one free market principles to time management, such as how it encourages its trainer(s) and trainees (employees) to arrange whose time to participate every different kind of training program efficiently and effectively. So the organization and its trainer(s) and trainee(s) must need time to learn how to arrange time to participate every different kinds of training to avoid to influence their performance or/and productivity efficiency to be worse during they also need time to do their day-to-day job, due to training participation influences their time arrangement spending (opportunity cost) between their working hours/time and their training participation hours/time.

Thus, arrangement training program time can also give chance to let every trainee(s) and trainer to learn time management issue. Hence, I believe training reward is not only money reward (e.g. profit reward). It includes skill, knowledge upgrade, innovation strategy, policy changing, employee royalty, raising work efficiencies, improving work performance intangible reward. These reward must be the organizstion's future intangible reward. Hence, intangible reward must br more worth to compare tangible reward (profit) because the organization's employees will hav positive emotion or happy mood to serve whose organization if the training program can satisfy all of their psychological needs for long term.

Hence, a small company is arranging only one trainer may have a reasonable reason to require a quick training program decision, but larger firms are playing lottery game to need time spending to decide a training arrangement which is required or not. It is not to their advantage to withdraw the training program offer immediately. They must need spend time to decide whether one training program is required or not.

If they do wrong decision to reject the training program, it is possible to bring future serious economic loss. It can include intangible loss, such as loe efficiency, and low productivity, worse efficiency , waste working time, low employee royalty and bad mood, instead of money (profit) loss. So, large companies must need to spend time to decide whether very training program is worth to be needed to train their employees.

- Can train employees raise efficiency ?

For robot society case, if future our society will be a robot society, based on high technology that high technology can fully replace human beings and workers. Hence, it brings this question: Do any robot manufacturing organizations or applying robot tools to assist productivity organizations need training courses to raise employee individual manufacturing effort to learn how to apply robot tools to assist them to manufacture any products or learn how to manufacture robots to sell ?

Hence, when all artifiacts discovery as well as new technology are created by human intellection. We will achieve outstanding results higher than we expected , such as organization's innovation expectation, if organizations lead and manage correctly their intellection. No one doubts knowledge can manage everything.

Knowledge is a competitive advantage at any level: individual, organizational and country. In today's more competitive society, employees should learn for better knowledge skills and better performance. So, such as (AI) artificial intelligent industry development cost. I believe every organization must need arrange suitable training programs to raise their employees‘ efficiencies, productivities and performance by any kinds of (AI) training courses knowledge.

Such as (AI) development case, it proves that employee training of (AI) learning apply knowledge is one of the best ways to accumulate knowledge , use knowledge , update knowledge as well as transfer it to other people in the either (AI) tool applying or (AI) product manufacturing development organization. It is essential to pay more attention to managing the (AI) training knowledge process.

Such as the (AI) development industry, by instilling knowledge is the best way to convert a manual worker into a white collar worker and into a knowledge work, such as one white collar accounting clerk who needs to learn how to apply robot tool to assist he/she raises whose accounting productive efficiency or one vehicle manufacturing worker needs to learn how to apply robot to raise whose efficiency to manufacture any kinds of vehicles for whose employers when their employers accep to adopt robot technology to assist their employees to work to achieve raising productivities and efficiencies aim. So, (AI) training courses may be needed to satisy the employers' innovation needs when they choose to apply (AI) technology to assist their employees to work efficiently to do their day-to-day jobs.

Considerately, training courses skills have the ability to help employees to learn how to manage themselves. The ability of problem solving and decision making, as well as continuing earning consciousness during they need to work with (AI) tools as the same time in every working day in habit. Hence, training courses must have economic worth when the organizations need to apply robots (artificial intelligent tools) (AI) assistanc to raise whose every employee efficiency and productivity and work performance.

Consequently, when society accepts robots technology can be applied to assist any organization's employee to raise whose productivity, efficiency or performance. Then, I believe (AI) training courses will be accepted to be needed to every innovative orgaanization. It proves training can arise intangible and tangible rewards or benefits to every future innovative organization, when they accept (AI) tools assistance to their traditional inefficient worker production method. So, it seems training programs will have it's worth to assist any organization innovation or development to achieve long term benefits.

● Training Super Talent Human Methods

Want a Superior Workforce? How to Develop a High-Performance Workforce ?

A superior workforce is one that is collectively better than an average workforce. It often includes employees who are smarter, faster, more creative, harder working, insightful, aware of the competition, and autonomous. They are daily contributors to a harmonious workplace that emphasizes accountability, reliability, and contribution.

If your goal is a superior, high-performance workforce that is focused on continuous improvement, you need to manage people within a framework that focuses on performance management and development.To achieve this, there are seven components you need to implement. They work together to create a superior, high-performance workforce. Create a checklist to implement these components and to make sure you are following through regularly.

1. Hiring

Create a documented, systematic hiring process. Ensure that you hire the best possible staff for your superior workforce:

· Define the outcomes desired from the people you hire.

· Develop job descriptions that clearly outline the performance responsibilities.

· Develop the largest pool of qualified candidates possible. Search via professional associations, social media networking sites such as LinkedIn, online job boards, personal contacts, employee referrals, university career services offices, search firms, job fairs, newspaper classifieds, and other creative sources when necessary.

· Devise a careful candidate selection process that includes culture match, testing, behavioral interview questions, customer interviews, and tours of the work area.

· Perform appropriate background checks that include employment references, employment history, education, criminal records, credit history, drug testing, and more.

· Make an employment offer that confirms your position as an employer of choice.

2. Defining Goals

Provide the direction and management needed to align the interests of your high-performance workforce with your organization's goals and desired outcomes:

· Provide effective supervisors who give clear direction and expectations, provide frequent feedback, and demonstrate the commitment to staff success.

· Company direction, goals, values, and vision should be communicated frequently and in memorable ways when possible.

· Provide a motivating work environment that helps employees want to come to work every day.

· Provide an empowering, demanding, commitment-oriented work environment with frequent mention of company goals to support your high-performance workforce.

3. Reviewing Progress

Hold quarterly performance development planning (PDPs)

meetings to establish aligned direction, measurements, and goals:

· Performance and productivity goals and measurements that support your organization's goals should be developed and written.

· Personal development goals should be agreed upon with individual employees and written. These can range from attendance at a class to cross-training or a new job assignment.

· Most importantly, progress on the performance development goals is tracked for accomplishment. Central tracking by Human Resources ensures the development of the entire workforce.

4. Feedback

Provide regular feedback to employees that lets them know where they stand:

· Effective supervisory feedback means that people know how they are doing daily, via a posted measurement system, verbal or written feedback, and meetings.

· Develop a disciplinary system to help people improve areas in which they are not performing as expected. The system is written, progressive, provides measurements and timelines, and is regularly reviewed with staff members.

5. Employee Recognition

Provide a recognition system that rewards and recognizes people for real contributions:

· Provide equitable pay with a bias toward variable pay using such methods as bonuses and incentives. Whenever possible, pay above market.

· Develop a bonus system that recognizes accomplishments and contributions.

· Design ways to say "thank you" and other employee recognition processes such as company periodic anniversary remembrances, spot awards, team recognition lunches, and more. You are limited only by your imagination.

· Despite the rising cost of health care insurance, which you may need to share with your employees, provide a continually improving benefits package.

6. Training

Provide training, education, and development to build a superior, high-performance workforce:

.Employee retention and education begins with a positive employee orientation. Employee orientation should give new hires a complete understanding of the flow of the business, the nature of the work, employee benefits, and the fit of his or her job within the organization.

· Provide ongoing technical, developmental, managerial, safety, lean manufacturing, and/or workplace organization training and development regularly. The type of training depends on the job. Some experts recommend 40 or more hours of training a year per person.

· Develop a procedure-based, cross-training matrix for

each position that includes employee skill testing and periodic, scheduled, on-the-job training and demonstration of capability, for most hands-on jobs.

· Provide regular management and leadership training and coaching from both internal and external sources. The impact of your frontline people on the development of your high-performance workforce is critical.

· Create jobs that enable a staff person to do all the components of a whole task, rather than pieces or parts of a process.

· Develop a learning organization culture through such activities as "lunch and learn," reading books as a team (book club), attending training together, and by making the concept of continuous learning an organization goal.

· Make a commitment to both providing and tracking the accomplishment of the developmental activities promised in the PDPs.

7. Employment Termination

End the employment relationship if the staff person is not working out:

· If you have done your job well—effective orientation, training, clear expectations, coaching, feedback, support—and your new staff person is failing to perform, termination of employment should be swift.

· View every termination as an opportunity for your organization to analyze its hiring, training, integrating, support, and coaching practices and policies. Can you improve any aspect of your process so the next new employee succeeds?

· Perform exit interviews with valued employees who leave. Debrief the same as you would a termination situation.

· Use an employment ending checklist to make certain you have wrapped up all loose ends.

Training method can be applied to employees. Similarity, training method can be also applied to super-athlete sport man.How to Grow a Super-Athlete ? I believe that training must need to grow a super-Athlete. I shall indicate how and why training is needed to grow a tennis super athlete sportman.

The future of tennis training?

A quick analysis of this talent map reveals some splashy numbers: for instance, the average woman in South Korea is more than six times as likely to be a professional golfer as an American woman. But the interesting question is, what underlying dynamic makes these people so spectacularly unaverage in the first place? What force is causing those from certain far-off places to become, competitively speaking, superior?

So even here, at the core of one of the globe's brightest talent blooms, the question of that talent's source remains enigmatically tangled, perhaps as much of a mystery to those who nurture these athletes as it is to the rest of us. It's enough to make you wish for a set of X-ray glasses that could reveal how these invisible forces of culture, history, genes, practice, coaching and belief work together to form that elemental material we call talent — to wish that science could come up with a way to see talent as a substance as tangible as muscle and bone, and whose inner workings we could someday attempt to understand.

However, basketball or tennis sport men, talent is not one main factor cause their super skill raising. Training is one important factor causes their super skill raising. "This is a new dimension that may help us understand a great deal about how the brain works, especially about how we gain skills."

Its very inertness is why the first brain researchers named their new science after the neuron instead of its insulation. They were correct to do so: neurons can indeed explain almost every class of mental phenomenon—memory, emotion, muscle control, sensory perception and so on. But there's one question neurons can't explain: why does it take so long to learn complex skills?

"Everything neurons do, they do pretty quickly; it happens with the flick of a switch," Fields said. "But flicking switches is not how we learn a lot of things. Getting good at piano or chess or baseball takes a lot of time, and that's what myelin is good at."

To the surprise of many neurologists, it turns out this electrical tape is quietly interacting with the neurons. Through a mechanism that Fields and his research team described in a 2006 paper in the journal Neuron, the little sausages of myelin get thicker when the nerve is repeatedly stimulated. The thicker the myelin gets, the better it insulates and the faster and more accurately the signals travel. As Fields puts it, "The signals have to travel at the right speed, arrive at the right time, and myelination is the brain's way of controlling that speed."

"What do good athletes do when they train?" George Bartzokis, a professor of neurology at U.C.L.A., had told me. "They send precise impulses along wires that give the signal to myelinate that wire. They end up, after all the training, with a super-duper wire — lots of bandwidth, high-speed T-1 line. That's what makes them different from the rest of us."

It also left me thinking about the clusters on the talent map. Specifically, wondering whether these places quietly possess myelin-accelerating factors: i.e., forces and conditions that promote what Fields would call "circuit optimization." Might those factors help explain the success of these superior athletes?
Hence, I feel that training is one important factor to manufacture super sport man and super employee. Talent is not the important factor to manufacture super sport man and super employee.

● The talent management skill
raises organizational development
and motivation of employees

When human primitive society is farming primary industry, farmers are only using hand to grow any kinds of plants, vegetable, fruit , rice to sell. Then, the farming work system was organized in primary forms using simple tools and with the least expertise and with division of duties in farm tasks. But in developed farming society, the farming work division is complicated, the farming duties are specialized, and the use of advanced farming technology, such as one farming vehicle can replace farmers' hand to grow any kinds of plants on farms.
The science of growing technology can help any plants to grow in fast speed and kill any animals, they can hurt plants to grow easily. This is good example of human talent technique development in farming industry. It can increase any kinds of plants growing of efficiency in fast speed and

short time growing in order to raise plants, fruit food productivies.

If human talent technique can be applied to our business society. Can human talent technique help any organization job characteristics raising efficiency and intrinsic motivation is more for the employees that are satisfied with their growth, and the employees with more experience were more satisfied with supervisor and collegues.

How can organizations apply talent management technique to raise work quality of the employees and their attempts? If any organizations hope to raise employee motivation. They need to concern how to change any job forms of content, job process to be more attractive. In order to achieve employees motivation more efficiently. For example, if the organization's employees can be motivated by more payments, fewer work hours, and suitable work condition. This kind of organizational talent management method ought bring employees motivation can be increased through providing independence and responsibility of the employees. The question concerns: Which factor or which factors motivate each employee in any organizations? Because every organization has different characteristics and different job title and duty. Some every organization factors motivate employees, they ought be different. Every organization ought focus on why individuals choose certain behavioral alternatives for satisfaction of needs in order to seek what factor(s) can increase its employees' motivation. Hence, if the organization has high degree of job motivation and satisfaction. The organization can predict the organizational commitment positively. So, it seems that one high degree of job motivation an satisfactory organization can bring high employee productivities turnover.

Organizational strategic talent method aims to create an accessible source of talents for adapting the right individuals with the right jobs and the right time based on the strategic purposes of business. Because the lack of talent is the biggest obstacle on the lack is a kind of major strategic advantage. Hence, any organization managers must need to know how to manage talents. How to use the individuals and how strategically to place them in proper position. Managers must design the situation to have the maximum knowledge and information, innovation and effort. And identify and discover whom are talents scarce and underdeveloped resources, how to seek talented employees. Such as talent labor market, it has key factors influence the efficiency of entering the labor market. These factors are the analysis of the current labor market situation and the rational preference of specialization. The active search and the talent employees interviewing, talent employees labor market search, these components are any organizations' talent recruitment essential method, if they hope to recurit any talented people to serve their organizations absolutely. Instead of talent recruitment factor, the other factors influence organizational success. They may include: Whether the organization has implemented feedback surveys, sensitivity training, management network, practical research, and training the techniques of improvement of intrapersonal relationships. So, those soft skills will be any successful organizations' essential talent management methods. So, organizations can not neglect any one of these factors in order to employee talented people to serve their organizations effectively.

- What is strategic talent management skill?

Strategic talent management skill can maximize the competitive advantage of an organization's human capital, this talent management is even more significant to be needed in nowadays organizational management, e.g. how to develop a talent pool of high potential and high performance to fill the organizatons' any roles as well as how to develop in differentiated human resource strategy to facilitate filling these positions with competent and to ensure all employees are talent to continue commitment to the organizations.

It is important to note that key positions are not necessarily restricted to the top management team (TMT), but also include key positions at levels lower than the TME and many vary between operating units and time. The reason is because any organization ought not need a stable top position, and this top position ought may be variable any time.

For one bank organization example, it ought not only CEO top position. It ought follow its market need to change CEO position, e.g. sometimes the bank may have more than one CEO position, e.g. share selling division CEO, housing loan division CEO, investment division CEO. Moreover, the lower position , such as manager can also increase to two or more, e.g. house loan division can have one CEO manager two housing loan department managers, even more. If the house loan division needs to increase staffs number to do any loan administration, loan applicaion and loan confirmation tasks in the house loan clients number busy time. So, bank top management CEO and lower management manager positions number can not ought keep only one. It is one wrong talent management strategy. It ought follow the client number to decide how to increase the right employees number in order to decide whether the bank's any department ought employ one CEO or manager position or more in order to solve the bank clients need number. Because if the bank only have one CEO and manager to manage their department. They will feel difficulty, if employees and bank clients number are increasing suddenly. They will feel busy and feel stressful. So, the bank ought need to decide whether the only one CEO and one manager to every department in busy time. It is suitable to its any departments to cooperate efficiently. Because if its any one department's management is inefficient, then it will influence employee performance and client dissatisfaction. So, the bank talent management method is that any time changes CEO and manager number to any department. Hence, organizational talent management depends on employees, clients number , market need, labor market supply factors.

- Talent in the world of work meaning

Talent in the world of work concerns talent management , high performers, high potentials and talent workforce segmentation. Talent should refer to a person's recurring patterns of thought, feeling or behavior that can be productivity applied. The sum of a person's abilities, his or her intrinsic gifts, skills, knowledge, experience, intelligence, judgement, attitudes, character and drive. Talent can be considered as a complex employees' skills, knowledge, cognitive ability and potential. Employees' values and work preferences are also of major importance, a select group of employees, those that rank at the top in terms of capability and preference, rather than the job, times commitment, willing to do the job, times contribition finding meaning and purpose in their work.

Hence, a talent person or worker who ensures the competitiveness, and future of a company as specialist or leader, through his organizational job specific qualification and knowledge , his social and methodical competencies, ans his characteristic attributes , such as eager to learn or achievement oriented. A talent person or worker has these characteristics: competence, knowledge, skills and values required for today' and tomorrow's job, right skills, right place, right job, right time and contribution , finding meaning and any nowadays talent person's characteristics.

Does talent refers to people (subject) or to the characteristics of people (object) ? Is talent more about performance, potential , competence, or commitment? Is talent a natural ability or does it relates more to further improving through practice? Talent is typically associated with athletes (e.g. Olympians, exceptional coaches, extraordinary teams, musicians of extraordinary ability, singers with incredible voices). It is commonly understood as above-average ability for a specific function or range or functions. Rather than corresponding to " normal" ability, talent is considered a special ability that makes the people who posses, develop and use it in the specific area of their talent.

Consequently, talent is often meant to excellent performance in a given performance domain. But in working society, talent has another meaning, i.e. people posses special skills or abilities. For job advertisement in which talent refers to potential applicants (e.g. talent wanted).

Talent s as a kind of natural ability, more than training to own personal skills capacity. In general, talent person owns a unique mix of innate intelligence or brain power, and a certain degree of creativity or the capacity to go beyond estabished stereotypes and provide innovative solutions to problems in his everyday life more easily to compare

common people.
In general, common people or student or worker can be taught to own skills and knowledge to learn easily. But , talent has characteristics much more unique. Therefore, talent is impossible to learn or teach easily. It is the person innate nature owns, talent can not really managed by any persons or organizations easily, because talent is always a function of experience and effort, e.g. an excellent sport person can be trained to be one excellent sport skillful talent person, even he has not one talent sport skillful person to any kinds of sport, e.g. riding bicycle, sport. If the sport person is not excellent in riding bicycle sport, but if he has a good trainer, he can teach good riding bicycle method or skill to be trained him to be one riding bicycle sporter. Then, for a long time riding bicycle learning perios, he will have possible to be one talent riding bicycle sport person. So, in some situaton, one non-talent learner will be trained to be one talent learner, if the trainer has good skills and methods to teach the trainee, such as riding bicycle sport case, it is not all riding bicycle sport person is one talent sport man. Their excellent riding bicycle skills need to be trained to raise their riding bicycle skills. Then, their talent on riding bicycle skills will be raised to be performed in possible. So, for sport man case, talent is not natural, talent sport man (trainee) is trained by trainer.
Hence, creating a talent person, it depends on these factors: The right place, the right position, and/or the right time. Such as the riding bicycle sport trainee case, he needs have right riding bicycle learning school , e.g. riding bicycle facility, good quality bicycle and large bicycle indoor spor place to let the bicycle sport trainee to learn. Then, he also needs a good trainee to learn. Then, he also needs a good bicycle teaching trainer , he can teach good riding bicycle

skill and fast speed riding and safe riding knowledge to let him to ride his bicycle in the riding bicycle competitive games in the fastest speed safely in order to win his riding bicycle competitors.

Finally, right time is also important factor, if in the time, the riding bicycle trainee has physical body hurt challenge or poor emotion psychological challenge. These factors will influnce his riding bicycle learning performance or abilities in order to achieve the best performance level. So, he needs to wait the time, he has good physical health and good emotion psychological time, then he can learn his riding bicycle trainer's riding bicycle knowledge and skill easily. Hence, one talent sport man needs have above these thress basic requirements: right place, right position, right ime in order to achieve the talent sport man training in success.

Training Super Talent Human Methods

● Non-training method creates talent young people

Want a Superior Workforce? How to Develop a High-Performance Workforce ?

A superior workforce is one that is collectively better than an average workforce. It often includes employees who are smarter, faster, more creative, harder working, insightful, aware of the competition, and autonomous. They are daily contributors to a harmonious workplace that emphasizes accountability, reliability, and contribution.

If your goal is a superior, high-performance workforce that is focused on continuous improvement, you need to manage people within a framework that focuses on performance management and development.To achieve this, there are seven components you need to implement.

They work together to create a superior, high-performance workforce. Create a checklist to implement these components and to make sure you are following through regularly.

1. Hiring

Create a documented, systematic hiring process. Ensure that you hire the best possible staff for your superior workforce:

· Define the outcomes desired from the people you hire.

· Develop job descriptions that clearly outline the performance responsibilities.

· Develop the largest pool of qualified candidates possible. Search via professional associations, social media networking sites such as LinkedIn, online job boards, personal contacts, employee referrals, university career services offices, search firms, job fairs, newspaper classifieds, and other creative sources when necessary.

· Devise a careful candidate selection process that includes culture match, testing, behavioral interview questions, customer interviews, and tours of the work area.

· Perform appropriate background checks that include employment references, employment history, education, criminal records, credit history, drug testing, and more.

· Make an employment offer that confirms your position as an employer of choice.

2. Defining Goals

Provide the direction and management needed to align the interests of your high-performance workforce with your organization's goals and desired outcomes:

· Provide effective supervisors who give clear direction and expectations, provide frequent feedback, and demonstrate the commitment to staff success.

· Company direction, goals, values, and vision should be communicated frequently and in memorable ways when possible.

· Provide a motivating work environment that helps employees want to come to work every day.

· Provide an empowering, demanding, commitment-oriented work environment with frequent mention of company goals to support your high-performance workforce.

3. Reviewing Progress

Hold quarterly performance development planning (PDPs) meetings to establish aligned direction, measurements, and goals:

· Performance and productivity goals and measurements that support your organization's goals should be developed and written.

· Personal development goals should be agreed upon with individual employees and written. These can range from attendance at a class to cross-training or a new job assignment.

· Most importantly, progress on the performance development goals is tracked for accomplishment. Central tracking by Human Resources ensures the development of the entire workforce.

4. Feedback

Provide regular feedback to employees that lets them know where they stand:

· Effective supervisory feedback means that people know how they are doing daily, via a posted measurement system, verbal or written feedback, and meetings.

· Develop a disciplinary system to help people improve areas in which they are not performing as expected. The system is written, progressive, provides measurements and timelines, and is regularly reviewed with staff members.

5. Employee Recognition

Provide a recognition system that rewards and recognizes people for real contributions:

· Provide equitable pay with a bias toward variable pay using such methods as bonuses and incentives. Whenever possible, pay above market.

· Develop a bonus system that recognizes accomplishments and contributions.

· Design ways to say "thank you" and other employee recognition processes such as company periodic anniversary remembrances, spot awards, team recognition lunches, and more. You are limited only by your imagination.

· Despite the rising cost of health care insurance, which you may need to share with your employees, provide a continually improving benefits package.

6. Training

Provide training, education, and development to build a superior, high-performance workforce:

.Employee retention and education begins with a positive employee orientation. Employee orientation should give new hires a complete understanding of the flow of the business, the nature of the work, employee benefits, and the fit of his or her job within the organization.

· Provide ongoing technical, developmental, managerial, safety, lean manufacturing, and/or workplace organization training and development regularly. The type of training depends on the job. Some experts recommend 40 or more hours of training a year per person.

· Develop a procedure-based, cross-training matrix for each position that includes employee skill testing and periodic, scheduled, on-the-job training and demonstration of capability, for most hands-on jobs.

· Provide regular management and leadership training and coaching from both internal and external sources. The impact of your frontline people on the development of your high-performance workforce is critical.

· Create jobs that enable a staff person to do all the components of a whole task, rather than pieces or parts of a process.

· Develop a learning organization culture through such activities as "lunch and learn," reading books as a team (book club), attending training together, and by making the concept of continuous learning an organization goal.

· Make a commitment to both providing and tracking the accomplishment of the developmental activities promised in the PDPs.

7. Employment Termination

End the employment relationship if the staff person is not working out:

· If you have done your job well—effective orientation, training, clear expectations, coaching, feedback, support—and your new staff person is failing to perform, termination of employment should be swift.

· View every termination as an opportunity for your organization to analyze its hiring, training, integrating, support, and coaching practices and policies. Can you improve any aspect of your process so the next new employee succeeds?

· Perform exit interviews with valued employees who leave. Debrief the same as you would a termination situation.

· Use an employment ending checklist to make certain you have wrapped up all loose ends.

Training method can be applied to employees. Similarity, training method can be also applied to super-athlete sport man.How to Grow a Super-Athlete ? I believe that training must need to grow a super-Athlete. I shall indicate how and why training is needed to grow a tennis super athlete sportman.

The future of tennis training? A quick analysis of this talent map reveals some splashy numbers: for instance, the average woman in South Korea is more than six times as likely to be a professional golfer as an American woman. But the interesting question is, what underlying dynamic makes these people so spectacularly unaverage in the first place? What force is causing those from certain far-off places to become, competitively speaking, superior?

So even here, at the core of one of the globe's brightest talent blooms, the question of that talent's source remains enigmatically tangled, perhaps as much of a mystery to those who nurture these athletes as it is to the rest of us. It's enough to make you wish for a set of X-ray glasses that could reveal how these invisible forces of culture, history, genes, practice, coaching and belief work together to form that elemental material we call talent — to wish that science could come up with a way to see talent as a substance as tangible as muscle and bone, and whose inner workings we could someday attempt to understand.

However, basketball or tennis sport men, talent is not one main factor cause their super skill raising. Training is one important factor causes their super skill raising. "This is a new dimension that may help us understand a great deal about how the brain works, especially about how we gain skills."

Its very inertness is why the first brain researchers named their new science after the neuron instead of its insulation. They were correct to do so: neurons can indeed explain almost every class of mental phenomenon—memory, emotion, muscle control, sensory perception and so on. But there's one question neurons can't explain: why does it take so long to learn complex skills?

"Everything neurons do, they do pretty quickly; it happens with the flick of a switch," Fields said. "But flicking switches is not how we learn a lot of things. Getting good at piano or chess or baseball takes a lot of time, and that's what myelin is good at."

To the surprise of many neurologists, it turns out this electrical tape is quietly interacting with the neurons. Through a mechanism that Fields and his research team described in a 2006 paper in the journal Neuron, the little sausages of myelin get thicker when the nerve is repeatedly stimulated. The thicker the myelin gets, the better it insulates and the faster and more accurately the signals travel. As Fields puts it, "The signals have to travel at the right speed, arrive at the right time, and myelination is the brain's way of controlling that speed."

"What do good athletes do when they train?" George Bartzokis, a professor of neurology at U.C.L.A., had told me. "They send precise impulses along wires that give the signal to myelinate that wire. They end up, after all the training, with a super-duper wire — lots of bandwidth, high-speed T-1 line. That's what makes them different from the rest of us."

It also left me thinking about the clusters on the talent map. Specifically, wondering whether these places quietly possess myelin-accelerating factors: i.e., forces and conditions that promote what Fields would call "circuit optimization." Might those factors help explain the success of these superior athletes?

Hence, I feel that training is one important factor to manufacture super sport man and super employee. Talent is not the important factor to manufacture super sport man and super employee.

- The talent management skill raises organizational development
and motivation of employees

When human primitive society is farming primary industry, farmers are only using hand to grow any kinds of plants, vegetable, fruit , rice to sell. Then, the farming work system was organized in primary forms using simple tools and with the least expertise and with division of duties in farm tasks. But in developed farming society, the farming work division is complicated, the farming duties are specialized, and the use of advanced farming technology, such as one farming vehicle can replace farmers‘ hand to grow any kinds of plants on farms.

The science of growing technology can help any plants to grow in fast speed and kill any animals, they can hurt plants to grow easily. This is good example of human talent technique development in farming industry. It can increase any kinds of plants growing of efficiency in fast speed and short time growing in order to raise plants, fruit food productivies.

If human talent technique can be applied to our business society. Can human talent technique help any organization job characteristics raising efficiency and intrinsic motivation is more for the employees that are satisfied with their growth, and the employees with more experience were more satisfied with supervisor and collegues.

How can organizations apply talent management technique to raise work quality of the employees and their attempts? If any organizations hope to raise employee motivation. They need to concern how to change any job forms of content, job process to be more attractive. In order to achieve employees motivation more efficiently. For example, if the organization's employees can be motivated by more payments, fewer work hours, and suitable work condition. This kind of organizational talent management method ought bring employees motivation can be increased through providing independence and responsibility of the employees. The question concerns: Which factor or which factors motivate each employee in any organizations? Because every organization has different characteristics and different job title and duty. Some every organization factors motivate employees, they ought be different. Every organization ought focus on why individuals choose certain behavioral alternatives for satisfaction of needs in order to seek what factor(s) can increase its employees' motivation. Hence, if the organization has high degree of job motivation and satisfaction. The organization can predict the organizational commitment positively. So, it seems that one high degree of job motivation an satisfactory organization can bring high employee productivities turnover.

Organizational strategic talent method aims to create an accessible source of talents for adapting the right individuals with the right jobs and the right time based on the strategic purposes of business. Because the lack of talent is the biggest obstacle on the lack is a kind of major strategic advantage. Hence, any organization managers must need to know how to manage talents. How to use the individuals and how strategically to place them in proper position. Managers must design the situation to have the maximum knowledge and information, innovation and effort. And identify and discover whom are talents scarce and underdeveloped resources, how to seek talented employees. Such as talent labor market, it has key factors influence the efficiency of entering the labor market. These factors are the analysis of the current labor market situation and the rational preference of specialization. The active search and the talent employees interviewing, talent employees labor market search, these components are any organizations' talent recruitment essential method, if they hope to recurit any talented people to serve their organizations absolutely. Instead of talent recruitment factor, the other factors influence organizational success. They may include: Whether the organization has implemented feedback surveys, sensitivity training, management network, practical research, and training the techniques of improvement of intrapersonal relationships. So, those soft skills will be any successful organizations' essential talent management methods. So, organizations can not neglect any one of these factors in order to employee talented people to serve their organizations effectively.

- What is strategic talent management skill?

Strategic talent management skill can maximize the competitive advantage of an organization's human capital, this talent management is even more significant to be needed in nowadays organizational management, e.g. how to develop a talent pool of high potential and high performance to fill the organizatons' any roles as well as how to develop in differentiated human resource strategy to facilitate filling these positions with competent and to ensure all employees are talent to continue commitment to the organizations.

It is important to note that key positions are not necessarily restricted to the top management team (TMT), but also include key positions at levels lower than the TME and many vary between operating units and time. The reason is because any organization ought not need a stable top position, and this top position ought may be variable any time.

For one bank organization example, it ought not only CEO top position. It ought follow its market need to change CEO position, e.g. sometimes the bank may have more than one CEO position, e.g. share selling division CEO, housing loan division CEO, investment division CEO. Moreover, the lower position , such as manager can also increase to two or more, e.g. house loan division can have one CEO manager two housing loan department managers, even more. If the house loan division needs to increase staffs number to do any loan administration, loan applicaion and loan confirmation tasks in the house loan clients number busy time. So, bank top management CEO and lower management manager positions number can not ought keep only one. It is one wrong talent management strategy. It ought follow the client number to decide how to increase the right employees number in order to decide whether the bank's any department ought employ one CEO or manager position or more in order to solve the bank clients need number. Because if the bank only have one CEO and manager to manage their department. They will feel difficulty, if employees and bank clients number are increasing suddenly. They will feel busy and feel stressful. So, the bank ought need to decide whether the only one CEO and one manager to every department in busy time. It is suitable to its any departments to cooperate efficiently. Because if its any one department's management is inefficient, then it will influence employee performance and client dissatisfaction. So, the bank talent management method is that any time changes CEO and manager number to any department. Hence, organizational talent management depends on employees, clients number , market need, labor market supply factors.

- Talent in the world of work meaning

Talent in the world of work concerns talent management , high performers, high potentials and talent workforce segmentation. Talent should refer to a person's recurring patterns of thought, feeling or behavior that can be productivity applied. The sum of a person's abilities, his or her intrinsic gifts, skills, knowledge, experience, intelligence, judgement, attitudes, character and drive. Talent can be considered as a complex employees' skills, knowledge, cognitive ability and potential. Employees' values and work preferences are also of major importance, a select group of employees, those that rank at the top in terms of capability and preference, rather than the job, times commitment, willing to do the job, times contribition finding meaning and purpose in their work.

Hence, a talent person or worker who ensures the competitiveness, and future of a company as specialist or leader, through his organizational job specific qualification and knowledge , his social and methodical competencies, ans his characteristic attributes , such as eager to learn or achievement oriented. A talent person or worker has these characteristics: competence, knowledge, skills and values required for today' and tomorrow's job, right skills, right place, right job, right time and contribution , finding meaning and any nowadays talent person's characteristics.

Does talent refers to people (subject) or to the characteristics of people (object) ? Is talent more about performance, potential , competence, or commitment? Is talent a natural ability or does it relates more to further improving through practice? Talent is typically associated with athletes (e.g. Olympians, exceptional coaches, extraordinary teams, musicians of extraordinary ability, singers with incredible voices). It is commonly understood as above-average ability for a specific function or range or functions. Rather than corresponding to " normal" ability, talent is considered a special ability that makes the people who posses, develop and use it in the specific area of their talent.

Consequently, talent is often meant to excellent performance in a given performance domain. But in working society, talent has another meaning, i.e. people posses special skills or abilities. For job advertisement in which talent refers to potential applicants (e.g. talent wanted).

Talent s as a kind of natural ability, more than training to own personal skills capacity. In general, talent person owns a unique mix of innate intelligence or brain power, and a certain degree of creativity or the capacity to go beyond established stereotypes and provide innovative solutions to problems in his everyday life more easily to compare common people.

In general, common people or student or worker can be taught to own skills and knowledge to learn easily. But , talent has characteristics much more unique. Therefore, talent is impossible to learn or teach easily. It is the person innate nature owns, talent can not really managed by any persons or organizations easily, because talent is always a function of experience and effort, e.g. an excellent sport person can be trained to be one excellent sport skillful talent person, even he has not one talent sport skillful person to any kinds of sport, e.g. riding bicycle, sport. If the sport person is not excellent in riding bicycle sport, but if he has a good trainer, he can teach good riding bicycle method or skill to be trained him to be one riding bicycle sporter. Then, for a long time riding bicycle learning perios, he will have possible to be one talent riding bicycle sport person. So, in some situaton, one non-talent learner will be trained to be one talent learner, if the trainer has good skills and methods to teach the trainee, such as riding bicycle sport case, it is not all riding bicycle sport person is one talent sport man. Their excellent riding bicycle skills need to be trained to raise their riding bicycle skills. Then, their talent on riding bicycle skills will be raised to be performed in possible. So, for sport man case, talent is not natural, talent sport man (trainee) is trained by trainer.

Hence, creating a talent person, it depends on these factors: The right place, the right position, and/or the right time. Such as the riding bicycle sport trainee case, he needs have right riding bicycle learning school , e.g. riding bicycle facility, good quality bicycle and large bicycle indoor spor place to let the bicycle sport trainee to learn. Then, he also needs a good trainee to learn. Then, he also needs a good bicycle teaching trainer , he can teach good riding bicycle skill and fast speed riding and safe riding knowledge to let him to ride his bicycle in the riding bicycle competitive games in the fastest speed safely in order to win his riding bicycle competitors.

Finally, right time is also important factor, if in the time, the riding bicycle trainee has physical body hurt challenge or poor emotion psychological challenge. These factors will influnce his riding bicycle learning performance or abilities in order to achieve the best performance level. So, he needs to wait the time, he has good physical health and good emotion psychological time, then he can learn his riding bicycle trainer's riding bicycle knowledge and skill easily.

Hence, one talent sport man needs have above these thress basic requirements: right place, right position, right ime in order to achieve the talent sport man training in success.

● Building high performance culture talent management method
to organizations

Any human decision making can influence our organizations value. How our culture causes may influence how we can fall serve to our organization? Our organization culture can influence how we bring energy, creativity and enthusiasm to our organization value. So, it brings these questions concern how our organizational culture can bring high performance to our organization productivity , such as:

How can our talent management to our organization culture can bring consequence on increasing profits and shareholder value, attracting and keeping talented people, building brand loyalty, ensure that ethic corporate culture to achieve high performance. Also, how out talent management to our organization culture can help we deliver high quality , cost effective services and a sustainable society service. The key questions concern how building a high performance culture to our private and public sector organizations. We need to know that the culture of an private organization's source comes from its competitive advantage and brand differentiation, as well as the culture of an public organization source comes from its cost effectiveness and quality of services.

Hence one successful public and private organization cultures may bring these performance effects: values and behaviors drive cutlure, culture drives employee fulfilment, employee fulfilment drives customer satisfaction and mission achievement. Because any organizational staff's cultural behavior, their principles, ideas, or briefs that people (staffs) can influence organizational operation. For example, similarly, if the organization has potentially limiting value of bureaucracy, that it can cause rigidity and limit the free idea expression from any staffs. This organization cultural value will limit employees' personal value and poor financial peformance because it's organizational cultural value is not " open mind" or let employees have chance to share their opinions to discuss their company any issues very easily.

So, bureaucracy cultural value will be weakness to any organizations, e.g. some countries' government organization is bureaucracy cultural value. It can not innovate or raise or improve its government internal organization different departments' efficiencies very easily. But, it needs lone time to do any decisions . It is a bureaucracy organization's weakness or easy cooperation between the values of the culture of the organization and the personal values of employees, the final effect is low performance, which can further resultin low levels of staff engagement and poor quality of products and services. All these bureacucracy organization's long time decision making and messages need long time delivery factors can have a significant impact on the financial performance or low efficiency (inefficiency) of the organization or its ability to deliver services of low quality.

Hence, if the organization's culture is able to attract and retain talented individuals. This gives organizations a significant commercial advantage, especially when talent is in short supply. Strong brand values are always those with the strongest internal cultures. So, it has relationship between high cultures, brand differentiation, or retaining talented individuals and the successful is highly dependent on the culture that the leaders create.

Also, the culture that leaders create is highly dependent on the behaviors of the leaders and their relationship to other leaders in the organization, and their relationships with their employees. It explains that why organizations with strong , high performing cultures tend to replace their leaders by promoting from within, whereas low -performing cultures tend to replace their leader's with external candidates. The reason is because that by promoting from within, organization's good cultures are also to retain their successful leadership styles. However, organization's culture and desired leadership styles is one kind of management feeling from all employees and managers working behavior and attitude. Any organizations must need spend time to research what their organization culture is and what leaders desired leadership styles are.

How can we know our organization culture is suitable to let our low level and high level employees accept to work together? We can follow those change to judge whether our organization's culture is suitable organization culture. The change may include: A different way of doing. Doing what we do now, but doing it in a more efficient, productive, or quality -enhancing way, a different way of being. Transformation involves changes at the deepest levels of beliefs, values and assumptions. Transformation occurs when we are also be learnt from our mistakes, are open to a new future, and can let revise of the part mistakes.

Hence talent retension is critically important for all organizations for two main reasons: Turnover is expensive and top performers drive business performance. Turnover costs arise from the direct replacement costs of talent acquisition, the opportunity costs of vacant positions and time to productivity, in the result costing of business performance. Hence, one organization has good cultural value, it may have characteristics: The organization can have confidence to recruit the right people in the first place, it can improve the line manager's ability to manage, it can give employee's constrant feedback about clear, meaningful goals, it can empower employees to manage their own careers, it can continuously measure and improve retention strategies easily. All of these are any good cultural organization's characteristics.

Hence, talent managemen may a key aspect of human resources management strategy in any organizations? In this age of the rapily expanding knowledge-based economy, the quality of human resources has assumed crucial importance. This complex and demanding market environment has a demand for outstanding and talented with high development potential, being the lever of growth in shareholder value. The organization talent leader has attitude, a performance -oriented approach, the ability to persuade, teamwork, emotional intelligence, flexibility, a high tolerance to change, and highly developed specialist technical skills. However, it has relationship between developing talent people and good organizational culture. Because developing talent people and good culture, then it can develop talent people easily.

How can we know that the organization has good culture. Similarly, if we discover that the organization has many talent people are working, then we may assume that the organization has good organizational culture . We can follow how many employees' talent level, they own and they are working in the organization. The talent level can consist of these several points: Extraordinary intellectual skills (general and specialist), a creative attitude (originality, flexible thinking and acting, solving unconventional problems easily, and a high tolerance to risk, change , uncertainty) and a commitment to work (self-disciplined, persistent in pursuing goals, and hard-working). Hence, if the organization has many employees, who own extraordinary intellectual skills, a creative attitude, a commitment to work attitude. Then, I believe that the organization owns many talent suitable to let them to feel to work.

Hence, what is talent management cultural organization? A talent management cultural organization can ensure that talent people are attracted, retained, motivated and developed in line with the needs of the organization, i.e. the most valuable staff memebers, by creating conditions conducive to their potential development. So that they can be put to use for the company's operations for as long as possible, talent management is a set of activities taken vis-a vis personnel with outstanding talents to ensure their development and increase their operational efficiency, when immediately achieve corporate goals easily. A talent management cultural organization consists of searching for talents inside or outside the organization, undertaking special activities to enable their development, training and career path planning and ensuring that their remuneration is competitive with that of other organizations, talent management involves implementing a set of key activities as part od human resource management , when immediately applying more advanced methods and techniques.

Hence, one talent management cultural organization ought own above all these characteristics. A talent management cultural organization can reduce employee turnover number, they can keep talent people continue stay to work in their organization for long time. So, when the organization's workforce (employee leaving) turnove rate reduces, in special talent employees, then its high performers and employees with hard-to-replace skills, these group employees will continue work in their present employers for long time.

Similarly, any talent management cultural organization really can prove itself is one successful organization , it must need long time to learn or improve itself strategy in order to attract many talent employees choose itself organization to work. Hence," learning how to attract talent employee method", which is a important factor to influence whether the organization can be one talent management cultural organization in success.

How can a digital platform one online talent platform assist organizations to recruit talent people? Online talent platforms can ease a number of these dysfunctions by more effective connecting individuals with work opportunities. Labor markets are arriving in the form of digital platforms, the very same technologies that have reshaped the businesses and consumer environment in areas , such as e-commerce.

Online talent platforms are marketplaces and tools that can connect individuals to the right work opportunities. The size of their user networks expand the pool of possibilities, and their powerful search capabilities in an efficient and personalized way. These digital platforms are rapidly popular, acceptable to apply on online talent recruitment method for any organizations.

Talent online recuritment platforms can help companies transform or change the traditional recruitment way or method. They hire, train and manage their employees. All this online talent recruitment method can give better-informed decisions about human capital produce better business results. In additions, online talent recruitment platform could improve signaling about the skill that are actually in demand across the economy. As this information shapes decisions about education and training, the entire skills mix of the economy could adjust more accurately over time.

Online talent recruitment platforms can take form of websites mobile apps, or proprietary corporate systems. They gather a huge volume of information regarding both individual workers and employers or work projects, then synthesize this data to match individuals with job opportunities and produce better work outcomes.

One online talent recruitment platform is a digital tools that enable users (organizations) to post full time or part time jobs, create online resumes of individuals, search for talent or work opportunities, based on extended matching attributes, provide personal working experience and qualification data into company or worker reputations, skills, assess candidates‘ attributes, skills or fit, personalize onboarding, training and talent management optimize team formation and internal matching, determine the best options for training and skill development.

Hence, online recruitment talent management platform will be a good tool to any organizations' human resource department talent employee choice method to help them to select the most talent employee(s) to work in the right position and in right time. It can replace the traditional newspapers applicant recruitment method or outsoucing job agent applicant recuriment method or government labor department post recruitment method. When one organization has many employees, e.g. 100, even 1000,

10000 or more employees number. Online talent recruitment platform can help it to reduce to spend much time to choose whom are the right applicatns to apply the job position, because (artificial intelligence) AI technology can replace human's judgement ability, it's judgement accurate level may exceed to human judgement level to choose the right applicants to enter the next interview stage. So, it explains that why online talent recruitment platform can replace any organization's human resource department's CV sceening process. It is one good (AI) online recruitment platform to help any recruiters' CV sceening process to be avoided, when (AI) online recruitment CV screening platform method is invented to assist any large organizations' human resource department to reduce time and staff nervous to do every applicant's CV screening activity. This is one good talent management application and recruitment and selection method to any large organizations' large human resource recruitment process.

Among young people are potential philosophers, artists, writers, entrepreneurs, whether training method is one important factor to create or manufacture any one of young peole to be super talent person successfully in our society. Some psychologists or behavioral scientists or doctors believe that formal educational (school) training is only the important method to train super talent young people. But, other some psychologists or behavioral scientists or doctors , they argue that formal educaiton (school) training is not the main method to create any one super talent young person in our society.Otherwise, they also feel that non-formal educaiotn method will be easily to create or manufacture one real super talent person in our society nowadays.

I agree the later professional groups' view point any more. I believe that the young person himself/herself free learning attitude factor is the most influential method to attract any one capacity within the young person to be one super talent person in society in possible more. The super talent young people can discover or seek whether what the real capability, they own
in success. They have these same characteristics: They can spend time to attempt to seek whether what their talent capability may own in order to develop their talent capabilities. Moreover, they do not need any teachers to teach how they may discover their talent capabilities in success in classrooms. Otherwise, they accept to spend their extra non-schooling time to seek whether what kind of talent capabilities , they may own in habit. Because when they feel what kind of talent capabilities that they may own in possible, then they will have habitual behaviors to be creative and innovative to their specialized talent undiscovered capabiliities often. Due to their accumulative time creates and innovates and concentrate on learning their one kind of talent capability, then they can enhance their the ability of non-formal education learning experience method to create or upgrade or raise the kind of their talent capabilities easily.

The question concerns: How do these common young people not need training method to create or innovate or raise
their talent capabilities to become one super talent young person in success? In fact, any one super talent person, he/she
must be common person in past long time before. It depends on whe he/she can discover or seek whether what the real talent capability that he/she may own in order

to upgrade or raise himself/herself this kind of talent capability in success. Even, when he/she knows or ensures that this kind of talent capability , he/she has owned really. He/she also needs long time to learn in order to upgrade or raise this kind of talent capability. SO, any one super talent young person must need long time to learn the kind of capability in order to be the kind of capability super talent young person.

Hence, it explains why school formal educaiton can not train any super talent students focus on one kind of capability in success. Schools can only provide one group students classroom learning environment to train any one common lazy student to be hard student to attempt to earn high grade to each subject in order to graduate to seek any kinds of occupation in achievement in our society. Otherwise, any one super talent owning one kind of capability at least person, who will not need school learning training method.

They need to spend time to discover any one kind of talent capability , that they own in possible in order to attempt to learn how to upgrade or raise their this kind of themselve owning capability to be raised to super talent capability level, e.g. some super talent pinano music tool player, when he/she feels interest to play pinano music tool, then he/she will spend extra time to learn how to play this kind of pinano music tool in order to create many good pinano music to let audiences to listen. They do not feel formal education training method can raise their playing pinano music tool skill. They choose to learn from themselves at home in their extra time. So, non formal education learning method has more successful chance to train one common pinano music player to be one super talent pinano music player to compare formal education learning method consequently.

Hence, young people need know how to create and innovate their capacities by themselves. This positive attitude is important in enhancing young peoples' innovative and creative potential in ways that are relevant to employability. It seems that non-formal learning method can support innovation and creativity in young people to their undiscovered capabilities to be upgraded or raised. Any countries government need to spend time to invest non-formal education method to raise young people to discover and learn what their talent capabilities are. The non-formal eduational talent young capabilities plan aims and strategies and outputs may include as below:

It's goals is investment in non-formal learning , leadning to increased capacity for innovation and creativity in young people in ways relevant to employability,enhancing user-freindly and efficient procedures and methods for recognition of non-formal learning in the development of innovation and creativity skills.

Targets set with indicators to provide signs of progress achievement. The implementing strategies can support non-formal education workers, especially youth workers, who work directly with young people, to raise the quality of provision, such as improving the recognition and validation of non-formal learning, providing (AI) artificialintelligent , robust and accessible tools and resources to support the talent young people capabilities discovering work. Developing partnership working relationship
between business and the formal education and non-formal sector, closing the gap between requirements of the labour market and the contribution of no-formal school learning, enhancing entreprensurial skills in young people.

In conclusion, non-formal school or non-formal training learning method or student himself/herself learning method can bring outputs to manufacture or create super talent young peron more easily to compare formal school learning method, e.g. one school teach 100 students, it won't create any one super talent capability of student easily. Otherwise, 100 young people who can spend extra time to learn how to upgrade or raise themselves owning capabilities at home. Any of one or more than one these 100 young people will have more chance to learn to become one super talent person who owns this kind of capability by himself/herself in success when he/she can accept to spend long time to learn by himself/herself. The reaons is that teachers can not persuade they discover to learn themselves capabilities more easier from themselves. So, one non-formal learning method can achieve these outputs, such as improved procedures and better use of non-formal learning method to measure and accredit non-formal learning, better use of methods to measure and access formal learning , improved provision of training and support for non-formal education workers, effective partnership between labour market and education (formal and non-formal) sectors, promotion of non-formal learning through financial support , technical advice, networks and databases, experiments to develop specific areas of practice. However, instead of young people need to spend time to discover what themselves interests or capabilities are and learn them, the another most importance to achieve non-formal education method successful factor is that the expert group will assist itself country government to work with formal and non-formal partners to ensure that ideas from social scientific research, literature, practice wisdom, policy and discovering any kind of capability consultation processes, inform understandings of any individual young person problems, situations and issues, as well as ideas about work that can enable desired outcomes and ways of monitoring and evaluating any individual young person himself/herself " capability discovery work" in order to create talent young person mission in success.

Employee Psychological Research

Employee satisfaction measurement

- How to measure employee satisfaction ?

It has close relationship between employee satisfaction and work motivation. The right staff can work in the right position which can affect the effective productivity of the company. Also, if employees feel satisfactory , then the company can have more chance to raise (increase) productivity, responsiveness, quality amd good customer service performance. However, if any company want employees to work efficiently, then which needs to know that one of the biggest internal strength of the organization is the relationship and communication between employees and the managers. Besides, the biggest improvement is also needed in the field of the financial rewards, because most of the employees are not showing high satisfaction to them.

Whether how to measure what the level of employee satisfaction is accepted to achieve the stable productivities? The main subjects will be leadership and motivaton to answer this question. For example, supermarket organization, whether which factors could be improved in the target work in supermarket organization every day? I shall assume it has perhaps to cause job dissatisfaction if the supermarket has only the power of money as motivator in supermarket organization. Any organization has its culture. As supermarket organization has also itself culture.

However, I believe that cultural traits that can affect the employee satisfaction in any supermarket organizations. Although, any supermarket organization has usually different departments to cooperate work together. Hence, if it has good organizational culture to make different departments, e.g. store, food, wine, stationery, clerical, counter etc. departments staff who can have good communication to work in comfortable cultural supermarket environment together, then its staff can have more ability to achieve the best work performance. How to solve this department cultural difference of challenge, I suggest any supermarket needs have good HRM plan to control its department's employee behaviors.

Human resource means the staff who work in a organization and the contribution who make with whose skill, knowledge and competence. The most important successful factor of knowledge based economy in which intelligent organizations are the key aspects of economic growth in the global economy. Why does organization need to satisfy employee needs? Because any staff trend to change working places often, any staff can change their workplaces to gain more respect and to feel more valued in their jobs. So, it can avoid staff turnover (leaving) whose organization very easy if the employer can satisfy whose staff needs. Thus, human resource plan is needed to achieve policies, recruiting and selecting work force, training and development, workplace planning, ensuring fair treatment of employees, ensuring equal opportunities, assessing the performance of employees, managing employee welfare, providing a counseling service for employees, managing the payment and rewards systems, supervising health and safety procedures, disciplining individuals, dealing with dismissal or promotion, negotiation, ensuring the legality of organizations etc. concerning about managing employees' positive psychological issues, in order to build positive emotion to them.

● How can leaders satisfy employee needs?
Any organization needs have good leaders because leaders act to provide satisfaction or more likely to offer means of satisfaction to whose team members. Leaders don't necessarily motivate. A successful leader understands the needs of the others and persuades them to act in a certain way. A good leaders can make whose workers see that following the views of the leader's workers will get the most satisfaction out of their work. However, a person can be motivated without leadership. But leadership, however, can't succeed without the motivation of the follower's side. If a staff has the feeling that who can perform a higher level job, himself/herself who have the motivation to attend courses or train in another way to be able to perform at the required higher levels.

Douglas Mc Gregor's famous classification of theory x versus theory y is applicable for leadership approaches. In general, any staff has two kinds of psychological characteristics of either theory x person or theory y person. Theory x assumes that in general most staff find working distasteful and usually avoid doing it if it is possible . That is why most staff must be controlled and directed, even threatened to perform the way the organizational goals will be reached. Theory x also assumes that staff want to be controlled and directed rather than take responsibility and that staff lack ambition. Otherwise, theory y on the other hand, is more likely to have roots in the recent knowledge of human behavior. It assumes that physical and mental effort in work is as natural as play or rest. So, leaders need to judge whether whole managing staffs (team members) who belong to theory x or theory y kind of staff. Then, who will have more accurate method to lead whose team members easily.

What level of satisfaction to the organization's staff can achieve the best performance. I feel that when the organization can reach the willingness level to be told the extent to which any one of staff has motivation and commitment or self-confidence to accomplish a certain task. So, the willingless level is the most satisfactory maturity level to achieve the best performance psychological factor to any organization. Because of the maturity satisfactory level of employees is high, the employees are both willing and able to do the tasks given more efficient. Otherwise, if the maturity satisfactory level is moderate, leaders can concentrate on the relationship and participate in the decision making and willing processes as workers are able but may be unwilling to complete their tasks. Only a little bit of enouraging is needed. Otherwise, if the maturety satisfactory level is low, workers are willing but may be unable to complete the tasks, so leaders must push to sell the tasks and let the workers do the rest or leaders must tell workers what to do.

In this supermarket organization case, if supermarket's gocery department and logistic department and clerical or cashier departments and fishing/meet etc. department whose employees' maturity satisfactory level is low, then it is possible that who are unable and unwilling to complete whose individual department daily tasks efficiently and these different department managers need to concentrate on both relationship and task aspects to raise whose maturity satisfactory level to be moderate level, even the high level in order to achieve the best performance.

Leaders also need to concern staff job satisfaction issue. Job satisfaction is the reflection of a good treatment. It also can be considered as an indicator of emotioned well being or psychological health, even job satisfaction can lead to behavior by an employee that affects organizational functioning. Furthermore, job satisfaction can be a reflection of organizational functioning. Why can job satisfaction influence any organizational performance? The reason is some people like to work and who find working is an important part of their lives. Some people on the other hand find work unpleasant and work only because who have to do support their lives. However, job satisfaction tells how much people like their job. Job satisfaction is the most studied field of organizational behavior. It is important to know the level of satisfaction at work for many reasons and the results of the job satisfaction studies. In the workers' point of view, it is obvious that feel repected and satisfied at work, it could be a reflection of a good treatment. In the organization's point of view good job satistaction can lead to better performance of the workers which affects how the result of the organization to achieve its productivities for long term.

So, any employer or leader can not neglect whose staff what job satisfaction level to whose staff in any time. In general, if whose staff can not feel job satisaction, who will choose to leave whose current employer more easily.

Raising employee efficiency

- How does one company raise employee

efficiency

What makes one company more successful than another? It is possible to conern better products, services, strategies, technologies or perhaps a better cost structure.

However, the final source is the best staff performance of good productive factor, because it can cause these result, also employees who are engaged significantly outperform work group and who are tangible asset to raise the company's competitive advantage where employees are the differentiator, engaged employees are the ultimate goal. What factors can affect job satisfaction. I find that agency theory might be helpful to explain how organizations need to think of their human resource responsible in producing the output needed by organizations to meet shareholders value. Agency theory is concerned with issues related to the ownership of the firm when that ownership is separated from the day-to-day running of the organization. It assumes that in all but owner managed organizations, the owner or owners (known is agency theory as the "principle" of an organization must best authority to an agent -corporate management to act on their behalf) Shenkel, R. Gardner, C. (2004, pp. 57-59).

The principle recognises the risk, here and act on the assumption that any agent will look to serve its own as well as the principle interests as it fulfills it contract with that principal. However, this is not the situation in real life situation. As all agents are perceived to be opportunistic. Agency theory is therefore used to analysis this conflict in interest between the principal (shareholders of organizations) and their agents (leaders of these organizations). The agents in keeping with the interest of the shareholders and organizational goals turn to use financial motivational aspects like bonuses, higher payrolls, pensions, sick allowances, risk payments to reward and retained their staff and enhance their performance. However, given this perception, the principal in an organization will feel unable to predict an agent's behavior in any given situation and so brings into play various measures to do with incentives in other to tie employee's needs to those of their organization. However, the fundamental problem, dealt with is that drives or induces people to exploit their potential resources in the way they do in organization. The issue of motivation and performance are who positively related. By focusing on the financial aspect of motivation problem likes bonus system, allowances perks, salaries etc. I believe financial motivation and trying to Mallow's Basic needs non financial aspect why comes in when financial motivation has failed. So, employers need to evaluate the methods of performance motivation in whose organization in organizing some motivational factors like satisfies and dissatisfies will be used to evaluate how employees motivation is enhanced other, than financial aspects of motivation. I believe that with the changing nature of the work force, recent trends in development, information and technology, the issue of financial motivation becomes consent on one of the most important assets in an organization. The potential role of money is as conditioned reinforce and an incentive which is capable of satisfying needs and an anxiety reducer and serves to erase feelings of dissatisfaction.

In general, any organization can use performance or efficiency to measure its productivities. Such as, performance means the act of performing; of doing something successfully; using knowledge as distinguished from merely possessing it; a performance comprises an event in which generally one group of staff (the performer or performers) behave in a particular way for another group its staff.

Efficiency means the ratio of the output to the input of any system. Economic efficiency is a general term for the value assigned to a situation by some measure designed to capture the amount of waste or friction or other undesiable and undesirable economic feature present. It can also be looked as a short run criterion of effectiveness that refers to the ability of the organization to produce outputs with minimum use of inputs.

Why does employer need to know how to motivate whose staff? What is meaning of motivation? Motivation means as the psychological process that give behavior purpose and direction to behave in a purposive manner to achieve specific unmet needs, an unsatisfied need, and they will to achieve respectively. So, salary, job satisfaction, job goal , reward will be task -related motivation since goals direct staffs' thoughts and action. So, motivation to staff needs have these factors expected. For example, phychological needs are the bottom of the staff, such as foods, air, water and shelter. Any staff needs a salary that enable then to afford adequate living conditions. Then, staffs need safety, psychological needs. They need to work for a secure working environment free from any threats or harms and organizations can provide these need by providing employees, with safety working equipment e.g. hardhars, health insurance plans, fire protection etc. Next, staffs need social needs and the needed to be loved and accepted by other people. Esteem includes the need for self-respect and approval of others. Finally, self actualisation is the top psychological need, it is capable of being to develop the staff himself/herself full potential. The rationale holds to the point that self actualised employees repect valuable assets to the organization human resource.

Why do employers need to concern flexible working arrangement? Employers need to concern flexible working arrangement if who hope employees can raise productivities and efficiencies to achieve the best work performance. Flexible working describes any types of working arrangement that gives some degree of flexibility on how long, where and when employees work. Because employees need time to learn a familiar phase with workplaces, flexible working arrangements have been an option in many employment sectors for a long time, helping employment meets the changing needs of their customers and staff. The reasons include customers expect to have products and services available outside of the traditional 9 to 5 working hours; employees want to achieve a better balance of between work and home life and organizations want to meet their customers and employees needs in a way that enables them to be as productive as possible. Organizations need to produce any products and services of the right quality and at the right price, under constant pressure. To meet customers' demands, sometimes new ways of working have to be found to make the best use of staff and resources. Flexible patterns of work can help to solve those pressures by maximising the available labor and improving customer service.

At employers, organizations also have a duty of care to protect whose staff from risks to their health and safety, e.g. stress caused by working long hours or feeling pressure to need to balance work and home life. However, flexible working can help to improve the health and wellbeing of employees and by extension, reduce absenteeism, increase productivity, and enhance employee engagement and loyalty. Flexible working time includes per time works often used in hotels, restaurants, warehouses etc. flexitime. Mostly used in office based environments for staff below managerial level in public and private sector service organizations; annualised hours often used in manufacturing and agriculture where there can be big variations in demand throughout the year.

Thus, I feel the flexible working and work life balance benefits can include a more efficient and productive organization, a more motivated workforce, better retention of valuable employees, a wider pool of applicants can be attracted for vacancies, reduced levels of absence and increased customer loyalty and working hours that the best suit the organization, its employees and its customers applications of knowledge about how people as indicators and groups, act within the total organization, analyzing the external environment's effect on the organization and its human resources, missions, objectives and strategies. So, it concerns how to predict staff psychological feeling to learn how to motivate who to work efficiently.

Why does manager need to concern employee's individual diversity need? Also, manager needs to know each person is substantically different from all others in terms of their personalities, needs, demographic factors and past experiences and/or because who are placed in different physical settings, time periods or social surroundings. This diversity needs to be recognized and viewed as a valuabe asset to organizations. Selective perceptions may lead be misinterprectation of single event work or create a barrier in the search for new experience. Managers need to recognize the perceptual differences aiming the the employees and manage them accordingly. These whole person effects between the work life and life outside work and mangagement's focus should be in developing not only a better employee but also better person in terms of growth and fulment. If the whole person can be developed, then benefits will beyong the firm into the larger society in which each employee lives. Because individual's behavior are guided by their needs and the consequences that results from their acts. In case of needs, people are motivated not by what others think who ought to have but by what who themselves went. However, motivation of employee is essential to the operation of organizations and the biggest challenge faced by managers. Organizations ought give more opportunities to let employees who can contribute their talents and ideas because many employees actively seek opportunities at work to become relevant decisions the stay or leave the organization, also managers ought concern any employee's individual skills and abilities and to be provided with opportunities to develop themselves.

Organizational behavior theory

● What is system approach?

What is system approach? All parts of an organization interact in a complex relationship. Systems approach takes an across, the board view of people in organizations and analyses issues in terms of total situations and as many factor as possible that may effect people's behavior. Three theoretical frameworks, the cognitive behavioristic and social learning frameworks, the basis of any organizational behavior model. The cognitive approach is based on the staff and organization expectancy, demand and incentive concepts. Because staff behavior on the basis of the connection between stimulus and response in any organization. The social learning approach incorporates the concepts and principle of both the cognitive and behavioristic frameworks. In this approach, staff behavior is explained as a continuous interaction between cognitive is explained as a continuous environmental determinants. In the organizational behavioral model, there are some dependent variables like productivity, absenteeism turnover, job satisfaction, deviane absenteeism, turnover, organizational citizenship behavior etc. The reason of which staff try to understand. The cause of these outcomes like with some variables of individual, groups and individual level, these variables are called independent variables.

It seems different organizational workplace environments will influence staff's different variable causes to decide how to do whole daily behaviors, how to fit to work in the organization. So, any manager needs to know what every staff is individual characteristics to judge how to manager himself/herself. For example, if the staff is thoery x person, who will dislikes work and will avoid it if possible, who lacks responsibility, has little ambition and seeks security above all who must be controlled, threatened with punishment to get who to work. So, the manager's attitude is needed to control whom. Otherwise, if the staff is theory y person, who will feel work is as natural as play as rest. People are not inherently lazy,who have become the way is as a result committed, the staff has potential, under proper condition who learn to accept and seek responsibility, who has imagination creativity that can be applied to work, so manageer who is to develop the potential to the staff and help who release that potential toward common objectives.

Any organization depends on the external environment for two kinds of into outputs, which it transforms into outputs and then releases in the hope that external environment will accept them. First, human input, employees and natural resources. Second, non human inputs, e.g. equipment, information, raw materials. However, organization needs to adjust to environmental demands, e.g. customer complaints, market research, financial reports, in order to keep to improve performance easily.

How to raise organizational efficiency? As systems theory indicates organizational effectiveness and time is considered as one element of a larger system of number of elements. The organization takes resources (inputs) from the external environment, processes these resources and returns them in changed form (output). According to system theory, effectiveness criteria must reflect the entire input process, output cycle, not simply output and must also reflect the interrelationships between the organization and its outside environment. In relation to environmental circumstances organization passes through different phases of lifecycle like forming, developing , maturing and declining and the appropriate criteria of effectiveness must reflect the stage of the organization's life cycle.

The criteria of effectiveness are also time based short run (results of actions concluded in a year or less), intermediate run (when effectiveness of individual, group or organization is considered for a longer period, perhaps five years and long run for this the time frame is indefinite future. The four short run effectiveness criteria are quality, productivity, efficiency and satisfaction. Three intermediate criteria are quality, adaptiveness, efficiency amd satisfaction. The two long run criteria are quality and survival. So, any organization needs have effectiveness criteria because effectiveness criteria can reflect the stage is of the organization's life-cycle (which includes stages of growth, maturation and decline) and short, intermediate and long term perspectives. Quality means the total quality control rank among the most used programs to meet customers' changing demand. Hence, employee's indiviaual satisfaction will influence productivity. Because productivity reflects the relationship between the organization's inputs and outputs and measures of productivity include profit, sales, market share. For example, patients released, clients served concerns the relationship between employees' satisfaction and clients' overall satisfaction. When the employee feel more satisfactory, then who will work more efficient or who will serve the clients more pleasant. Then, the customers will have more chance to feel more satisfactory from the staff's individual service.

Efficiency is the ratio of outputs to inputs. It focuses on the entire input process output cycle, emphazing inout and progess. Measures of efficiency include rate of return on capital, or assets, unit cost, waste, downtime, occupancy rates and cost per patient/student etc. customers. Satisfaction meets employee needs. It recognizes the organization is as social system that benefit its participants. Measures of satisfaction include turnover, absenteeism and employee attitudes. Adoptiveness means the degree to which the organization can and does respond to internal and external changes. It relates to management's ability to sense environmental changes and changes within the organizaton. There are no specific measure of adaptiveness, but certain progress, e.g. employee training and career counseling increase its capacity to deal with it. Finally, development means the ability of the organization to increase its capacity to deal with environmental demand. So, if the organization hope to be survival in the long term, then it needs to achieve training programs and organizational development to be represent the organization's investment in survival.

Employee satisfaction methods

- How can satisfy to employees' needs ?

How can satisfy to employees? Because a high rate of employee is directly related to a lower turnover rate. Thus, keeping employees' satisfied with their careers should be a major priority for every employers. Reasons why employees can become discourages with jobs and design, including high stress, lack of communication within the organization, lack of recognition, or limited opportunity for growth. So, management need actively seek to improve these factors to avoid if who hope to lower turnover rate. However, some employee will often be feel bored with the work because there is no intrinsic motivation to succeed. Finding the daily same job duties can reduce the individual's motivation to succeed to raise desire to show up to work and to do the job well. In this case, the employee may continue to come to work, but whose efforts will be minimal.

Stress is another factor to cause low performance. Branham (2005) indicates that " it seems clear that one quarter to one half of all workers are feeling some level of dysfunction, sue to stress, which is undoubtedly have a negative improve on their productivity and the probability that they will stay with their employers."

However, stress can be caused by these factors, e.g. in the situation, when a company can't or won't supply the tools necessary to produce or work efficiently on the job. This produced higher stress levels because these workers are expected to perform at certain rates, yet who are unable to do so. This results in lower productivity and higher turnover because quotes can't be met by the employees. On staff knowing that management is able to provide the tools essential for the position is important to employee trusting the intentions of their employer.

Dissatisfaction with the job many come from sources other than stress or poor fit between employee and the job. Employers that are deemed unethical by workers because who appear to care about company revenues, rather than the employees that are working for them. In the result, the employer may lead to job dissatisfaction, and raise the company's turnover rate.

Lack of communication in the workforce is another major contributor to dissatisfaction. Bad communication leaves employees feeling disconnected from the organizations. This is detrimental to wellbeing of the company because when an employee feels neglected, who will trend to perform at a lower level because who feels unsure of whose position within the company and wonders what whose purpose is within the workplace. Also, employees may be unaware of how whose performance measures up to that of their co-workers and have no sense of who can improve. So, without communication, it becomes difficult for employees to make any progress in their efficiency. The employee may feel uncomfortable in the workplace, of who feel rarely be praises for the quality of whose performance. Finally, those factors cause the failure to provide employees with opportunities to grow within the company results in employee frustration to cause whose poor performance and low productivity.

Whether can bonuses increase raise employee satisfaction and team performance? In some occupations, I feel bonuses can raise staff performance, such as bonuses lead to happier and it can be used in the form of donations to charity organization or bonuses in the form of expenditures to pharmaceutical sales teams and sport teams organizations. However, employees are becoming more and more unhappy, more and more of time at work, hardly a formula for a healthy and productive workplace. In this increasingly negative environment, how can employers incentivize their employees to increase their happiness, job satisfaction, and job performance? Certainly, designing effective incentive schemes is a central challenge for a wide range of organizations form multi-national corporations to academic departments. Identifying the most effective strategies, a variety of incentive schemes and are suggested such as bonuses from fixed salaries to pay-performance from commission to end-of-year bonuses. It is based to assume that the best way to motivate employees is to reward them with money that who then spend on themselves. In general, existing methods of increasing workplace performance, including individual-based and team based bonuses schemes, which trend to reveal both benefits and unexpected cost. Whether the benefits of improving social life in the work phase can increase employee citizenship behaviors to satisfy the organization actual needs from these bonuses compensation schemes.

What is the effect of money on employee's job satisfaction and performance? On one hand, monetary bonuses have been found to have positive effects, increased productivity effort, performance and job satisfaction. Individual bonuses increase job satisfaction in part. On the other hand, individual incentives, such as large bonuses are often surprising ineffective increasingly employee morale and productivity. In an effort to prevent such negative competitive dynamic that can result from individual based-bonuses, organizations often change to incentivize employees for their collective performance, encouraging cooperation and teamwork rather than competition. Otherwise, in some cases, team based compensation schemes have been shown to raise this sense of cooperation between team members, inducing them to exert additional effort toward helping another worker to work together linked to employee morale and performance.

Whether bonuses can have a causal impact on employee. In fact, individual incentives, such as large bonuses are often surprisingly ineffective in increasingly employee morale and productivity. Also, rewarding individual employees can produce negative outcomes, as employees become reluctant to share information with others even at the expense of reduced output. In an effort to prevent such negative competitive dynamics that can result from individual based bonuses. Importantly, such increased cooperation due to interdependent rewards has been shown to improve team performance, suggesting that team based bonuses may be an effective means of improving employee social life. As with individual based bonuses, however team based bonuses offer important advantages, but also potential drawbacks. I suggest that prosocial bonuses can have a causal impact on employee satisfaction and performance, such that providing employees with money to spend on themselves.

How effective organizational communication can affect employee attitude, happiness and job satisfaction. Communication has been studied with regard to performance and job satisfaction, but the relationship with employee attitude and happiness has not been done in a higher education setting. The value of communication in an employee's choice to be happy is explained as it affects the individual, team and overall organizational culture.

Attitude and happiness have been recognized by communication examination of organizational culture and emotion in the workplace. For example, for frontline employees are needed have cheerful and positive in the face or any situation. So, it requires the owners, managers and supervisors communicate to whose team efficiently.

Communication with telecommuting or remote workers is a consideration that organizations must take seriously more than 24 million people were working remotely in 2008 year (World at work, 2009) and that number is steadily rising. Teleworkers report feelings of isolation, uncertainty, a lack of trust and lower organizational commitment with lower job satisfaction. Managers may not communicate the save way with remote workers as who do with employees who are in the workplace each day. Improve communication is important to hold employee engagement initiatives together, particularly in government public sector organizations must communicate throughout the entire cycle of planning, conducting and acting on engagement. So, I suggest some effective communication method to raise productivity and improve performance. Such as ensuring that employees understand their work expectation between their jobs and the organization's mission, meeting regularly with staff members, providing feedback as performance , as well as opportunities to grow and developing , even fail as a way to learn and holding employees accountable for performance, including with poor performance.

How to make a difference at work be more meaningful and purposeful workplaces. The workplace provides a wealth of opportunities and possibilities through which anyone can make a difference every day. Whether it's one person, one team or one organization, everyone has the capacity to create positive and meaningful change in their workplace in both small and large ways. How to foster the work motivation of individuals and team? Nowadays, some evidence supports claims that motivational programs can increase the quality and quantity of performance from 20 to 40 percent. Moreover, motivation can solve three types of performance challenges: first, staff are refusing to change often, second, allowing themselves to be distracted and not persist at a key task and/or third, treating a task as familiar, making mistakes but not investing mental effort and taking responsibility because of overconfidence.

Imagine that more than 50% of staff in your organization decided that from this point, who would work one extra day a work without an extra day of rest. What impact would their decision have on your organization's bottom line? What is the value of a 50% increase in performance by 100% of the workforce? Assuming that you may know some of the 50% , who do the minimum and a few of the 80% who could work much harder, do you think that there is anything that would convince people to work harder than who are now? Is it possible that half of your staff who admit that who could work much harder might actually decide to increase whose performance by 20% or more if they were adequately motivated? The best evidence suggests that highly significant performance increases are possible when motivational strategies are implemented (Clark & Estes, 2002).

- How to achieve work motivation strategy ?

Work motivation is the process that initiates and maintains goal-directed performance. Without motivation , even the most capable person will refuse to work hard. Thus, motivational performance gaps exist whenever staff avoid starting something new, resist doing something familiar, stop doing something important or attention to a less valued task, or refuse to work smart on a new challenges, instead use old familiar, but inadequate solutions to solve a new problem (Clark, 1998).

How can we make sense of such variety and get benefits as performance technologies? Is any given situation where we want to increase work motivation, we must determine what will convince staff to start doing something new or different increase their persistence at an important task and investment mental effort. The staff must believe that the motivator driving their enhanced performance will directly or indirectly contribute significantly to what who need to feel successful and effective. The motivator's work has to cost less than the value of the increased performance and it must meet both ethical and legal requirement. When it might appear that solutions have to be tailored to the different demands of individuals in a team. In the absence of a clear vision leading to work defined business and performance goals, people substitute their own goals and whose goals may not support the organization. So, it is important to ask about evidence for the benefit of all work rules and what might be cost of the rules more eliminated. What is gained by rules that staff can't take or eat in certain areas? Why can't they decorate their work space in ways that suit them? How much of staff's behavior must you control to achieve business goals? One way to motivate and staff and simplify organizational work processes is to eliminate all unnecessary rules, policies and procedures.

To learn how to motivate staff, we need to learn how to predict staff's individual psychological behavior. Organizational behavior is a scientific discipline in which large number of research studies and conceptual developments are constantly adding to its knowledge base.

It is also an applied science, in that information about effective practices in one organization is being extended to many others. Organizational behavior is the systematic study of human behavior, attitudes and performance within an organizational setting, drawing on theory methods and principles from such disciplines as psychology, sociology and cultural anthropology to learn about individual perceptions, values, learning, capacities and actions when workings in groups .

Nowadays, why employees hope employers can give them to enjoy well life balance. The reasons may include care commitments to children or elderly relatives, education commitment that limit availability at times of the week/month/year, duties and/or interests outsid of work, needing to be available for people making a greater sense of well being and reduced stress levels. How to arrange flexible working in organization? For example, an employer may be thinking about introducing annualised hours in order to increase productiom levels to meet infrequent rises in demand because who can work well where, there are peaks in works, the workforce is required to be available with little notice. The employer could decide to meet these increases in demand by introducing overtime because it provides flexibility to meet fluctuations and it could be a smaller change to the organization than annualised hour. However, there are many different forms of flexible working. Flexible working can cover the way working hours are organised during the day, week or year. It can also describe the place of work, such as homeworking or the kind of contract, such as a temporary contract. Anyway, flexitime can operate in different ways depending on business need. On the one hand, there may be a system to allow employee to build up additional hours, which can be used to leave early, come in late, or take longer periods off with early, come in late, ot take longer periods off, with approval from line management. An example of this might be an assembly line or call centre where staffing must be scheduled to meet customer demand. For example, an employer needs to extend the hours that whose business is open to 8 AM to 8 PM, but can't afford the extra overtime. how to manage flexitime approach could help provide the additional hours, reduce staff numbers at quiet times and minimise the need for overtime. Employer may benefit from the opportunity to travel outside of peak hours and/or accommodate personal responsibilities, such as the school runs part time work is the must common types of flexible working. It's potential benefits include customer demands on be met and machinery can be caused more efficiently if part time workers cover lunch breaks/ evening shifts and weekends, the working day can be arranges around caring responsibilities and/or other commitments, employees can continue to work increasing whose own leisure time. But part time work also have potential challenges, such as increase in training, increase in administrative and recruitment costs, e.g. recruiting two part timers could longer than one full times and providing a continuous level of service may be difficult.

Overtime is normally hours that are worked over the usual full time hours. It can be compulsory or voluntary . A recognized system of paid overtime is more common with hourly paid staff than salaried staff. Potential benefits include that employer can provide flexibility to meet fluctuations in demand, short term labor shortage without having to recruit extra staff overtime. Even with premium payments, is often less costly than recruiting and training extra staff or buying extra equipment. However, overtime work has also potential challenges, include when working excessive overtime can affect an employee is performance health and home life. It can result in higher absence levels and unsafe working practices.

Job sharing is a form of part time working where two or more people share the responsibility for a full time job. They share the pay and benefits in proportion to the hours each works. They share the pay and benefits in proportion to the hours each works. Job shares may work split days, split weeks or alternate weeks. it's potential benefits include that if one job sharer is absent, due to illness or holiday, the other can carry on with at least half the work, who can help meet people demand , e.g. both shares being present when workloads are heavy, a wider range of available, who can help people with caring responsibilities and/or other commitments to continue working. It is potential challenges also include extra induction, training and administration cost, replacement may be difficult if one job sharer leaves, added responsibility on supervisors/ managers, who must allocate well fairly and ensure that the job shares communicate effectiveness. If the shared role involves managing on supervising staff can find it is difficult working for two managers.

Shift work is a pattern of work in which one employee replace another doing the same job within a 24 hour periods. Shift workers normally work in crews, which are groups of workers who make up a separate shift team. it's potential benefits include it can reduce costs by using equipment more intensively and taking advantage of cheaper off peak. It's potential challenges include it can increase wage and labor costs, it can disrupt employees' social and domestic lives, it can upset employees' body and affect an employee's performance and health.

Employers ought concern employee engagement issue. Different professions have their own specific, which need to be addressed during the engagement building process. For example, for hospital workers, safety issue is of a high importance as who deal with different kinds of sicknesses, whereas for teachers or conselors, ths issue of stress and emotional exhaustion many be of more importance.

To learn how to satisfy employees, content with their work experience, was a good formula for success, as a satisified employees, who wanted to stay with a company, contributed to the workforce stability and productivity. However, satisfied employees may just meet the work demands, but this won't lead to higher performance. In order to compete effectively, employers need to go beyond satisfaction. Therefore, modern organizations expect their employees to be full of enthusiasm to work. Other researchers state that employee engagements is the best fool in the company's efforts to gain on competitive advantages and stay competition. Though, the notion of engagement is relatively new, and it is already a hot managerial topic and it is rare to find an HR or managerial related acticle that doesn't mention employee engagement. These researchers agree that engagement creates the prospect for employees to attach closely with their managers, co-workers and organization in general and engaging environment is the environment when employees have positive attitude toward their job and are willing to do high quality job.

It seems that how to develop good engagement workplace environment can influence employees' satisfaction, then it can influence whose performance or productivity. So, they have close relationship. however, it is even harder to build engagement within the specific group of employees in the situation, when the knowledge about the specifics of their work-life is missing. Different occupations need have different engagement workplace environments and engagement methods to let employees to feel satisfaction. For example, engagement of administrative workers in the educational organizations is rarely studied and poorly understanding, even though these employees have a significant influence in the institution and the quality of their performance contributes to the quality of relationships with faculty students and the public. So, understanding the administrative personnel work life perception is important to educational organizations. How schools can implement engagement to achieve target to improve administration employees (administrative workers) whose performance, students, faculty public satisfaction and other organizational outcomes. Because whose performance is not save to factory workers to cause how many product quantities manufacturing per hour to calculate, whose need to use service quality to measure performance.

I feel it is better in the situation when organizattions have a better understanding of the administrative personnel work-life perceptions, it is easier for them to create appropriate engagement building tools. Such as, administration employees working at small sized education organizations are more engaged, and this might be due to the reason that they have better relationships with colleagues and experience a greater sense of belonging than their colleages from larger education organizatins. Futhermore, Johnsrud and Rosser (1999) also suggest that the smaller the institution, the more positive administrative workers moral and consequentially the higher chances for their engagement. Therefore, result of this study can be applied only to the educational institutions of the similar size. Furthermore, results of this study can't be used for similar organization in order contributions.

What factors can influence the engagement of administration staff. I feel that significant variables factors include: working conditions, job fit, role fit, time spent interacting with students and length of employment on campus. As some researchers working conditions were found to be a significant and positive factor influencing engagement, this means that better working conditions increase the chance that the employee will shoe in higher level of engagement person job fit was defined by Edwards (1991, as referenced in Kristof, 1996, p.8) as " the fit between the abilities of a person and the demands of a job , i.e. demands-abilities or the desires of a person and the attributes of a job needs supplies". Job fit also focuses more on the formal aspects of the work, when role-fit includes both established and new tasks, which core out in teams, as team members' roles include formal tasks as well as informal socially defined tasks. The only factor , which was found to have a negative influence on the engagement of administrative workers was employment history, meaning that the higher level of employees were working within an educational organizaton, the lower level of engagement who showing.

I shall recommend to measure the engagement level of employees and to find out the specific engagement that need to be improved, the quantitative research with questionnaires as the main source collecting data was needed to choose to any educational organizations. Because questionnaires can produce numberical data, which is a quantitative approach. The educational administrative workers can be compared with each other within the category of engagement and can point out the factors driving engagement, which need to be improved. These numbers are the basis for further analysis and recommendations. The factors, which can be chosen for the investigation, include meaningful job autonomy at work, performance feedback, institution development opportunities, organizational support, procedural justice, social support from colleagues, supervisory support, social climate etc. The reasons to choose these factors to investigate because the meaningful job can increase psychological meaningfulness for the employee and therefore increases engagement.The above factor meaningful job has been included in the list. Besides, job characteristics can increase meaningfulness for the employee and are positively rarely to job engagement. However, educational administrative workers‘ moral has an influence on their perception an attitude to the job. The same study pointed out that the moral of administrative workers in educational organization is influenced by number of factors, such as working atmosphere, relations with colleagues and supervisors. For example, social support from colleagues and supervisory support is concerned to moral issue. Social climate factor is concerned to reward and recognition issue.

Why employers need to concern employee moral issue. For example, any clinic organization has complex interpersonal relationships within the clinical domain and the critical issues are faced by nurses on a daily basis, indicate that morale, job satisfaction and motivation are essential components in improving workplace efficiency, output and communiction amongst staff. Drawing on educational , organizational and psychological research, that the ability to inspire morale, staff morale which is a fundamental indicator of sound leadership and managerial characteristics. These includes role preparation for managers, understanding internal and external motivation, how internal motivation to nursing staff and the importantce of attitude when investing in relationships. Because this factors can influence nurse performance. As the field of nursing, amongst money others, the concepts of developing emotional self-awareness in staffs, self-control, adaptability in initiating in management, and organization teamwork in social networks have been poorly applied. Despite this, it has been suggested that nurse and physican collaboration is one of three strongest predictors of psychological empowerment of nurses (Larrabee et. 2003).

Relationships on the ward can influence to nurse satisfaction and personal professionals are closely linked to self-esteem or person's own morale. So, morale of nurse occupation can influence performance to serve patients. In health care industries, how to create healthy working clinical environments and encourage nursing staff for leadership and management roles, the issues of morale and motivation need to become primary concerns in the ward setting. Because any nurse service will fill with dread, fear and anxiety to whose patients if who neglects to concern care morale. So, nurses need to concern motivating behavior and discourages pessimistic feelings and performance. The reality is that some people naturally posses a high level of this internal motivation, these who focus on the internal feelings of satisfaction who will attain despite any difficulties who face along the way. Exceutives are coached, athletes are coached, why not health care professionals? The nature of helping others through clinical care provision may preclude staff from asking for help themselves.

Has it relationship between boosting morale and improving performance in the nursing occupation? For example, healthy working environment and system may be assisted through the regularity of coaching key staff, e.g. nurses in hospitals need to create any clinic ward organizations. Clinical will environments with good retention, work satisfaction and high quality measures. Nurses can also learn how to self-coach be more self aware and develop themselves. In the nursing occupation, linking nurses' daily work to long term ambitions will impose their motivation, boost their self-confidence and assist them to function at a higher performance level. Coaching will also help staff recognise their own management styles, and identify their leadership strengths and areas for improvement. Because nursing work is frequently rewarded by patients' gratitude. Nurses within clinical settings often comment on the patients' capacity to say thank you and their appreciation of how nurses contribute to their well being. So, the success of their health care service. In fact, performance appraisal is ideally about recognising the direction an individual nurse wishes to pursue concern how health care moral behavior to nurses to achieve to satisfy patient's individual need to reduce complaint occurrences to build healthy clinic environment to let nurses to work enjoyable.

Why absenteeism will influence performance? Unscheduled absenteeism is a popular problem for U.S. employers, conservatively costing $3,600 per hourly employee per year and $2,650 per salaries employee per year, the majority of employers have limited ability to accurately and regularly track how much absenteeism is reducing their bottom line earning, effective absence management systems can track absenteeism, manage absence policies and work schedules, and control overtime, allowing management to reduce lost earnings, also reducing absenteeism will also help employers better meet production and service demands without requiring an increase in headcount. Commonly, the unschedules absenteeism rate in the U.S. hourly workforce is approximately 9% almost one in ten workers is absent when who woud be at work. There are considerble direct and indirect costs are increasing. Not only should managers be motivated to reduce absenteeism because of the excss costs, but without absence tracking tools, employers can't adequately estimate their accurated liabilities. However, absenteeism causing is probable due to poor health to the individual employee. So, who will perform poorly to influence whose productivity to be worse. Why is there such little focus on absenteeism, compared to other costs, health care or low productivity or poor service performance costs for example? So absenteeism can raise much different workforce related costs. The excess costs arise cause disruption to the business, make it difficult to deloy the workforce, and have a profound effect productivity, profit margins and poor employee morale.

However, improving employee health can at most, only reduce absenteeism by one-third, as two-thirds of absenteeism is caused with non-sickness (personal reasons, feeling of entitlement, family issues). In the result, the direct impact is reduced or poor delayed production or customers are not being served. How to solve absenteeism challenges? Generally, the employer was using a five day schedule, but demand was such that employees were asked to come in on the weekend on a regular basis. The employees disliked working, so many consecutive days with no time off, which led to very high absence rates. The shortages of employees results in demand not being met and customers were dissatisfied. The organization has to replace missing workers with other employees or contractors and pay overtime or higher rates. Overtime levels are 28% higher in facilities with low absenteeism. Excess staffing plan, such as headcount is higher than necessary in order to cover unplanned absences. For example, the employer routinely increased headcount by 13% on weekends to copr with extra absenteeism on a Saturday and Sunday. It is less usual for a salaried employee to be replaced when absent. Instead, the demands of customers (internal or external) are not met and depending on the employee's position in the company, the ability to create revenue may be affected. Excess absenteeism can also lead to increased health care cost, greater safety issues and accidents, high turnover, and poor morale or performance. To achieve significant reductions in the excess costs with absence, the manager must reduce the rate of absenteeism and the subsequent effect that absenteeism hasno the business. The first step is accuratey and efficiently tracking absenteeism rates and pattrens on a regular basis. The majority of organizations don't hae an automated means to track every instance of absence in one system and therefore lack the visibility necessary to address this business problem. Once the root causes of the problem are known. The manager can consider what steps need to be taken. There may include using rules engines and process automation to consistently enforce absence policies, compliance with union, state and rules, improving absence management technology and increasing employee satisfaction with the workplace, reducing overtime costs by selecting employee to cover for absence based on their competence, training and hours worked during the week, accurate reports of absenteeism , patterns over time and root causes.

In order to take full advantage of opportunities for business expansion and growth. Human assets investment strategy is very important to any organizations. For example, airport organization, it needs good employees serve to provide excellent customer services to satisfy the increase flight slots at airports. So good human assets investment strategy can drive focus on safety, innovation and globalization and create programs for motivating employees to enable them to fully demonstrate their abilities. Such as airport training is needed to be given by lecturers, include rank based and elective training to airport service industry. Methods are such as on site courses, supporting the career development to any airport different rank of staffs to promote on environment where individual employees can display their capabilities to the maximum possible extent in their repective roles. In special, giving women career training establishing a mentor system under which senior employees provide ongoing direction and support for junior and new employees and introducing role models through an intranet, supporting for working includes holding seminars for woman who are pregnant or on maternity leave and introducing a system or partical employment. As a result, the number of employee and nearly all of tem return to the workforce. Because airport service industry needs have a large female workforce, including cabin attendants and airport passenger service staff. Besides, airport service industry also needs to hire women for career track administrative and maintenance positions and flight crews and working to increase the percentage of women in management positions.

Better work life balance is also needed to satisfy airport service industry staff. Besides, airport service industry also needs to hire women for career track administrative and maintenance positions and flight crews and working to increase the percentage of women in management positions. Because airport job duty is common needed to be shift duty. Hence, the working time is flexible time to work when new employees decide to attribute to airport service career. However, due to many passengers need, so airport service workers need to work overtime hours. But, commonly, who do not hope to work overtime often. So, airport management needs to create an comfortable and enjoyable working environment in which each new or old employee can rethink whose own working style to contribute will help vitalize society, companies and individuals.

How to leverage technology to improve employee engagement? Nowadays, employee engagement has evolved from a relatively unknown trend to a term in common usage, which leads itself to a variety of forms and levels of understanding. Employee engagement is about the ability of leaders to inspire their people around the way forward at the desired pace, involving a planned communication effort that is integrated with all the other leadership and change activites. Employee engagement is the emotional commitment the employee has to the organization and its goals. However, technology can play an important role in making engagement a practical part of everyday work. As companies move towards a digital workplace, understanding the impact of technology on employee engagement is critical.

What is the digital workplace? The digital workplace is the digital environment in which staff work, and a place to find corporate knowledge. It includes a collection of election tools that enable productive, effective, work from anywhere. In the future, according to the workplace of the future survey by Teknion corporation predicted 88% of companies offer their workforce personal devices, such as smartphones and tablets. Nearly 90% of companies plan to increase their investment in productivity enabling technologies, such as voice activation and video conferencing by 20 15 year. Organizations are seeking the difital workplace as which search for ways to be more efficient, more collaborative and reduce their physical workplace to realizing higher levels of productivity with their workforce. So, it seems digital workplace can assist to raise performance. Two important reasons why new technology tools will be represent great return on investment for internal use with employees.

The first reason is technology helps us comment with and engage remote or disconnected employees, those with little or no computer or internet access during their work time . The second reason is peer-to-peer engagement and using technology can drive the generation of more ideas, which drives innovation and improvement to produce in any workplace. So, creating an actionable roadmap that fully technology in sny organization's staff engagement initiatives can improve bottom line performance. So, technology can assist organization to measure employee engagement, connect disconnected workers, envourage collaboration and social interaction.

I assure engagement lies in sound decision making and action, then driving good decision making and action should be a communicator's core strategy. Many communicators are already doing good work to drive action. Then, good decision making is driven, in part, by the availability f good information. Even employees who are less digitially connected at work can contribue great ideas that improve that work situation and organizational productivity. Examples, of ways technology helps to that such as: one employee posts about a project who is working on, another employee in an office on the other side ot the world sees the post and realizes who is working on a similar project. If the two teams combine their effort, who can solve the problem and the company gets a globl solution. So, corporate internet is a new digital workplace tools. To effectively solve challenge as making the right information available to the right people at the right time. Organizations must begin by clearly identifying the core types of information that must be shared to engage employee and bring about maximum organizational benefit.

What critical organizational information should all employees access? What types of knowledge are suitable for collaboration? What informational exist today and how are these pockets of information affecting business performance? When analyzing your environment for knowledge sharing, take the time to understand knowledge sharing objectives and how to get employees on information that empowers them to be more successful and therefore more engaged. Remember, anyone can serve in this knowledge management role as long as who are contributing relevant and engaging information.

When looking at any new technology to improve organization knowledge transfer and employee engagement for your employees you should conside the following questions: How does the proposed technology create for information sharing? Are they create for information sharing? Are they easy to use for people of all levels of the organization? How does the technology solution you are examing help employees get work accomplished? This is especially important when examining enterprise social technologies. How can the technology provide more information about company vision, people, business processes. How effectively does the technology support key organizational scenarios, such as identifying the best talent for a particular department or initiative? For example, hospital environment can give conversation about the patient benefits of a new in-room online information display at a hospital.

● How can influence organizational positive behaviors ?
Nowadays, there are key forces are affecting daily organizational behaviors and continuing challenges, such as staff structure (work relationship), technology (resources inputs)are needs to transform to with people work and affects the tasks that who perform, environment (internal and external) factors influence the attitudes of staff, affect working conditions and provide competiton for resources and power. So, based on these four forces, managers need to face the different challenges, such as managing chances in a global environment, managing ethical issues at work.

How to raise staff performance to satisfy clients' needs? Customer service and satisfaction is not limited to the private sector, public sector also needs , e.g. education reform, privatizatin, managed case. So, staff need have excellent performance to raise quality of service to satisfy students, patients etc. needs. Why organizations focus on customer satisfaction. Business monitor customer satisfaction in order to determine how to increase customer base, customer loyalty, revenue, profit, market share and survival. Besides, government needs to monitor monitor customer satisfaction to achieve citizen needs. What is customer satisfaction? Customer satisfaction can be experienced in a variety of situations and connected to both products and services. It is a highy personal assessment that is greatly affected by customer expectations, satisfaction also is based on the customer's experience of both contact with the organization , the moment of touth and personal outcomes. Private sector means it is as one who receives significant added value as well as public sector means it is to whose bottom line. However, customer satisfaction differs depending on the situation and the product or service. A client may be satisfied with a product or service on experience, a purchase decision, a salesperson, store, servicce provider or an attitude. So, staff performance can influence or client's decision to choose to buy the product or consume the service indirectly. For example, in hospital organization , patient surveys often ask customers to rate their providers and experiences in response to detailed questions, such as " How well did your physicians keep you informed?" These surveys provide "actions" data that reveal obvious steps for improvement.

Client satisfaction is highly personal assessment that is greatly influenced by individual expectation. In the public sector, the definition of client satisfaction is often linked to both the personal interaction with the service provider and the outcomes experiences by service users. For example, satisfaction with client worker interaction whether in person, by phone, or by mail or by email communication, satisfaction with the support payment , e.g. its accuracy and timeliness ans satisfaction with the effect of child support enforcement on the child. For hospital organization, staff performance need have these service quality factors to raise or improve whose service satisfaction experience to whose patients (clients), e.g. timeliness and convenience, personal attention, reliability and dependability, employee competence and professionalism, empathy, responsiveness, assurance, availability and tangible, such as physical facilities and equipment and the appearance of the personnel.

Satisfaction and engagement are two important distinct mesurements that provide valuable and actionable insights into the workforce. The problem is that how many organizations still view them as one and th same thing. As a result, they may be missing critical opportunities to foster the kind of workforce engagement that drives innovtion, boosts performance and increases competitive success. However, some organizations think which don't have to worry about engagement because turnover is how and employees seem satisfied when employee satisfaction is important to matintaining a positive work environment. Is it enough to help you retain top performers and drive bottom line impact? Probably not, by focusing more employee engagement, organizations are more likely to maintain a strong, motivated workforce that is willing to expand extra effort, drive business goals and deliver a return on HR's talent management investment. How to acheve actionable strategies for maximizing workforce engagement and subsequently, driving higher perfomance across the organization. It addresses critical questions, such as: Do you want satisfied employees or engaged employees? Which has a greater impact on the organization's bottom line? What are some proven techniques for addressing both satisfaction and engagement? Employee satisfaction can typically measued through surveys to gsther opinions about

HR related issues like bonus programs, benefits and work/ life balance. Som employee satisfaction can refer to how employees feel, that happiness about their job and conditions, such as compensation, benefits, work environment, career development opportunities. On the other hand, engagement refers to employees commitment and connection to work as measured by the amount of discretinary effort, who are willing to expand discretionary effort, who are willing to expand on behalf of their employer. High engaged employees go above and beyond the core responsibilities outlines in their job descriptions, innovating and thinking outside the box to move their organizations forward, much like volunteers are willing to give their fine and energy to support a cause about which they are truly passionate.

Can an organization have a satisfied employee who isn't engaged? Chances is an engaged employee is also a satisfied employee. However, it is certainly possible to have a satisfied employee a with a low engagement level. That's why focusing on satisfaction without addressing engagement is unlikely to foster the kind of expectional workforce performance that drives business results. Why do organizations need to care about their workforce engagement level? The primary goal of a business is to make money, even non profit organizations exist to fund their specific causes. Many studies have linked organizations need to get employees at all levels focused on driving revenue. Also which indicates to link employee engagement to workforce preference, customer satisfaction, productivity absenteeism, turnover. Employee engagement is a concept that is rooted in science and at the most fundamental level reflects the human condition itself.

It makes sense that this human motivation process would apply in the workplace just as in other areas of life. By motivating employees beyond basic satisfaction to achieve higher levels of engagement. HR professionals have more significantly impact business outcomes and drive bottom line results. Top-performing organizations understand that measuring employees' contentment levels and emotionl commitment to the organization on a regular basis can put them at a competitive advantage. Since satisfaction measures on employee happiness with current job and security opportunities to use skills and abilities, the organiztion's financial stability, relationship with immediate supervisor, compensation and benefits. In general, these factors can contribute to job satisfaction, such as job security, opportunities to use skills and abilities, organization's financial stability, relationship with immediate supervisor compensation and benefit, communication between employees and senior management, the work itself, autonomy and independence, management's recognition of employee preformance. However, fact engagement condition can have these difference with job satisfaction, such as relationship with co-workers, opportunities to use skills and abilities relationship with immediate supervisor, contribution of work to organization's business goal, meaningfulness of job, variety of work, overll corporate cultures. In general, staff tend to receive more pleasure and satisfaction from what who do if who are in jobs or roles that match both their interests and skills if staff feel who are making meaningful contributions to whose jobs, thei organizations do society as a whole, they tend to be more engages. Staff want to be recognized and rewarded for their contributions. Rewards and recognition come in many forms, including competitive compensation packages, a healthy work/life balance, or sales trips etc. benefits. So, lack of motivation will affect productivity. In addition, a number of point to low morale: declining productivity, higher incidence of absenteeism and friendness, increasing defective products higher number of accidents or a higher level of waste materials and scrapes. How much money (salary) will you give to your employee to satisfy whose needs? However, staff's needs differ some can be motivated by opportunity for growth and development, job security, good working condition moew than high salary.

In conclusion, as a manager, if you want to develop and encourage good employee performance, and good performance comes from strong employee motivation. But managers can't motivate employee. Motivation is an internal state, like emotions and attitudes, that only the individual can control. Managers can however, create a workplace environment to attempt to motivate staff. Nowadays, workplace is affected by a number of factors, includng a decreasing emphasis on money, an increasing amount of work, an increasing need to work together in teams. Hence, employers concern to consider these above different psychological factors which can influence employee's individual behavior to perform efficiently in any organization.

Reference

Branham, L. (2005). The 7 Hidden Reasons Employees Leave: How To Recognize The Subtle Signs And Act Before Its Too Late. New York, NY: Amacom.

Clark, R.E. (1998). Motivating Performance, Performance Improvement, 37 (8), 39-47.

Clark, R.E. & Estes, F. (2002). Turning Research Into Results: A Guide To Selecting The Right Performance

Solutions. Atlanta, G.A: CEP Press.
Johnsrud, L.K. and Rosser, V.J., 1999. College and University Midlevel Administrators:
Explaining and improving their morale. The review of higher education, 22(2), pp. 121-141.
Kristof, A.C. 1996. Person-organization fit: An Integrative Review of its conceptualizations, measurement and implications. Personnel psychology, 49(1), pp.1-49.
Larrabee J.H. Janney M.A., Ostrow C.L., Withrow M.L., Hobbs G.R. And Burant C. (2003) Predicting registered nurse job satisfaction and intent to leave., Journal of nursing administration, 33 (5), 271-283.
Shenkel, R. & Gardner, C. (2004), " Five ways to retain good staff", Family Management, Now-Dec. , pp.57-59.
World at work (2009). Telework trend lines. Retrieved from http://www.workingfromanywhere.org/News/Trend lines_2009.pdf

CHAPTER THREE

Lacking education and crime increasing ratio and recession relationship

Has it relationship between a recession and crime? To answer this relationship question, I shall explain what is macroeconomics. Then, you will give more clear understanding why and why recession will impact social crime behaviors to bre rasied in possible.

What is Macroeconomics? Macroeconomics is a branch of economics that studies how the aggregate economy behaves. In macroeconomics, economy-wide
phenomena are examined such as inflation, price levels, rate of economic growth, national income, gross domestic product
(GDP), and changes in unemployment.On the other hand, microeconomics looks at the behavior of individual actors in an economy (like people, households, industries, etc).

Macroeconomics is the branch of economics that deals with the structure, performance, behavior,and decision-making of the whole, or aggregate, economy, instead of focusing on individual markets.The two main areas of macroeconomic study are long term economic growth and shorter term business cycles.

There are two sides to the study of economics: macroeconomics and microeconomics. As the term implies,
macroeconomics looks at the overall, big picture scenario of the economy. Put simply, it focuses on the way the economy performs as a whole, and then analyzes how different sectors of the economy relate to one another to understand how the economy functions. This includes looking at variables like unemployment, GDP, and inflation.

Macroeconomists develop models explaining relationships between these factors. Such macroeconomic models, and the forecasts they produce, are used by government entities to aid in the construction and evaluation of economic policy, by businesses to set strategy in domestic and global markets, and by investors to predict and plan for movements in various asset markets.

Given the enormous scale of government budgets and the impact of economic policy on consumers and businesses, macroeconomics clearly concerns itself with significant issues. Properly applied, economic theories can offer
illuminating insights on how economies function and the long-term consequences of particular policies and decisions. Macroeconomic theory can also help individual businesses and investors make better decisions through a more thorough understanding of what motivates other

parties and how to best maximize utility and scarce resources.It is also important to understand the limitations of economic theory. Theories are often created in a vacuum and lack
certain real-world details like taxation, regulation and transaction costs. The real world is also decidedly complicated and their matters of social preference and conscience that do not lend themselves to mathematical analysis.

Even with the limits of economic theory, it is important and worthwhile to follow the major macroeconomic indicators like GDP,
inflation and unemployment. The performance of companies, and by extension their stocks, is significantly influenced by the economic
conditions in which the companies operate and the study of macroeconomic statistics can help an investor make better decisions and spot turning points.

- Specific Areas of Crime rate increasing ,due to poor macro economy environment influences

Macroeconomics is a rather broad field, but two specific areas of research are representative of this discipline. The first area
is the factors that determine long-term economic growth, or increases in the national income. The other involves the causes and
consequences of short-term fluctuations in national income and employment, also known as the business cycle, such as researching whether recession will cause crime rate rising issue.

Economic growth refers to an increase in aggregate production in an economy. Macroeconomists study economic growth with an eye toward understanding the factors that either promote or retard economic growth in order to support economic policies that will
support growth, development, and rising living standards. Growth is commonly modeled as a function of physical capital, human capital, labor force, and technology. So, when economic growth is raising, then unemployment rate will decrease in possible.

- Business Positive or negative Cycles and
the country's macro economic environment is good and bad relationship

A long term macroeconomic growth trends, the levels and rates-of-change of major macroeconomic variables such as employment and national output go through occasional fluctuations up or down, expansions and recessions, in a phenomenon known as the business cycle.

- Macroeconomics vs. Microeconomics , what can influence crime rate more?

Macroeconomics differs from microeconomics, which focuses on smaller factors that affect choices made by individuals and companies.Factors studied in both microeconomics and macroeconomics typically have an influence on one another. For example, the unemployment level in the economy as a whole has an effect on the supply of workers from which a company can hire.

A key distinction between micro and macroeconomics is

that macroeconomic aggregates can sometimes behave in ways that are very different or even the opposite of the way that analogous microeconomic variables do.Meanwhile, microeconomics looks at economic tendencies, or what can happen when individuals make certain choices. Individuals are typically classified into subgroups, such as buyers, sellers, and business owners. These actors interact with each other according to the laws of supply and demand for resources, using money and interest rates as pricing mechanisms for coordination

- What factors Cause of recessions ?

A recession implies a fall in real GDP. An official definition of a recession is a period of negative economic growth for two consecutive quarters. Recessions are primarily caused by a fall in aggregate demand (AD). This demand-side shock could be due to several factors, such as

· A financial crisis. If banks have a shortage of liquidity, they reduce lending – this reduces investment

· A rise in interest rates – increases the cost of borrowing and reduces demand

· Fall in asset prices. – negative wealth effect leads to less spending

· Fall in consumer/business confidence also exacerbated by negative multiplier effect.

· Appreciation in exchange rate – exports less competitive

· Fiscal austerity – when government cuts spending

Recessions can also be caused by

· Supply-side shock, e.g. rise in oil prices cause inflation and lower spending power.For example, in US, bank failures led to a fall in the money supply and deflationary pressures.Bank failures also caused lost confidence and discourage investment.

· Negative multiplier effect – initial fall in spending caused a knock on effect throughout the economy.

There were no automatic stabilisers. People were made unemployed and so started spending less themselves. For example , causes of UK recessions1981 recession was caused by:

1.High value of the pound which made exports more expensive and reduced demand for exports.This recession particularly impacted on British manufacturing. The Pound soared due to the discovery of North Sea Oil but also the high interest rates.

2.High-interest rates. In 1979, inflation in the UK was over 15%. The new Conservative government was committed to reducing high inflation they inherited. They pursued a tight monetary policy (higher interest rates) and tight fiscal policy (higher taxes, lower government spending. This reduced inflation but at the cost of falling spending, investment and output.interest-rates.

3.Tight Fiscal Policy. To control inflation the government were committed to reducing the levels of Government borrowing.

This was influenced by Monetarist beliefs that controlling excess government borrowing was essential to the economy. Therefore the government increased taxes which reduced the disposable income of consumers and therefore reduced consumer spending.

A recession occurs when there is a fall in economic growth for two consecutive quarters. However, if growth is very low there will be increased spare capacity and increased unemployment; people will feel there is a recession. A key feature in determining the rate of economic growth is the level of consumer and business confidence. If confidence was high then higher interest rates may not reduce demand. However if confidence is low and people fear they may be made unemployed, then they will start spending less, causing AD to fall (or increase at a slower rate). Therefore this shows that expectations are very important and it is possible for "people to talk themselves into a recession".

For an important feature of the UK economy is international trade case. Therefore the UK would be affected by a global recession. For example, a recession in the EU would cause a fall in demand for UK exports reducing our AD (EU accounts for 60% of our trade, therefore, is important). Also, a recession in other countries would affect economic confidence if people see the US in a recession they are worried and will spend less. However, a global recession may not cause a recession in the UK if domestic demand remains high.

Classical economists believe that any fall in Real GDP will be temporary and will end when labour markets adjust to the new price level. Classical economists argue that if there is a fall in AD then, in the short term, there will be a fall in real GDP However in the great depression of 1930s Keynes was very critical of this classical view he said that the long period of negative growth showed that markets do not automatically clear he argued that this was for various reasons.

1.Wages are sticky downwards. Firms should cut wages to reflect lower prices but in reality, workers are very resistant to cuts in nominal wages.

2.If wages were cut in response to unemployment, workers would have less spending power, therefore AD would continue to fall.

● Can economic crises bring rise in crime ?

Crime may peak during economic crises,
During periods of economic stress, the incidence of robbery may double, and homicide and motor vehicle theft also increase.While a consistent relationship between specific crimes and specific economic factors could not be established, the evidence shows that crime is linked to the economic climate. Such findings are consistent with criminal motivation theory, which suggests that economic stress causes an increase in criminal behaviour. The available data do not, however, support the theory of criminal opportunity, which suggests that decreased levels of production and consumption may reduce some types of crime, such as property crime, by creating fewer potential crime targets."The presence of youth gangs, the availability of weapons and potential targets, drug and alcohol consumption and the effectiveness of law enforcement all play a significant role in enabling or restraining overall crime levels",

● Relationship between a recession and crime

Criminologists say bad economies create more crime; economists say the opposite. But recent data reveals neither explanation is right. I've been wondering if hard economic times would cause people to commit more crimes. For example, areas with chronic poverty and unemployment tend to have high rates of child neglect and abuse. Child neglect and abuse greatly increase the risk of juveniles getting involved in crime.So areas with high rates of unemployment cop a double whammy. Their crime rates are higher because of the direct effect of unemployment and its long-term indirect effects as well.

Will the current recession produce an increase in crime? If the recession doesn't last long, there may be no effect at all.

But if the recession is deep and the pool of young long-term unemployed rises, there is every reason to expect an increase in crime. Moreover, if this happens, the effects may last a long while. The longer you are out of work, the harder it is to find a job, and the more attractive crime becomes as an alternative source of income. And what happens this recession depends on still more factors, the most important being the income that can be earned from crime e.g.selling illegal drugs. Many thoughtful observers think that we put too many offenders in prison for too long. For some criminals, such as low-level drug dealers and former inmates returned to prison for parole violations, that may be so. The difference results not from willingness to send convicted offenders to prison in many countries' legal system

● May Economic crises trigger rise in crime ?

For the same offense, you will spend more time in prison here than in England. Canada has seen roughly the same decline in crime,

but its imprisonment rate has been relatively flat for at least two decades. Another possible reason for reduced crime is that potential

victims may have become better at protecting themselves by equipping their homes with burglar alarms, installing extra locks on their cars, and moving into safer buildings or even safer neighborhoods.

We have only the faintest idea, however, about how common these trends are or what effects on crime they may have. Are their crime behaviors caused by economic crises ?

How to explain complex link between recession and crime? For In the Environmental Protection Agency example, required oil companies to stop putting lead in gasoline. At the same time, lead in paint was banned for any new home though old buildings still have lead paint, which children can absorb.

● Why do recessions at labour market entry matter for crime? So, why is it that youth who graduate during recessions are more likely to engage in crime?

Those who leave school during a recession, when youth unemployment rates are particularly high, struggle to find a job but do not yet have financial insurance. Knock-on effects can then lead to criminal careers for the young. On the other hand, those who have criminal records early on in their career may reduce their job opportunities and expected returns in the legal labour market see. However , I agrcc that crime is not only a feature of the teenage years — crime rates decrease with age but do not disappear subsequently. That suggests that there is an initial effect but criminal activity is somewhat persistent over the life cycle.

● Can that persistence be explained by the long-term impact of recessions?

A typical recession leads to a 5 percentage points higher than normal unemployment rate.What is the long-term impact of graduating into such conditions? Our empirical analysis of the link between crime and unemployment at labour market entry is based on a variety of US and UK cohort and individual level data sources. We exploit cohort level data for both countries to estimate the average effect of initial labour market conditions on criminal activity of cohorts that enter the labour market at different points in time, taking into account differences in cohort composition.

● Is crime Rates increasing during recessions?

A recession is a significant decline in economic activity spread across the economy, lasting more than a few months, normally visible in production, employment, real income, and other indicators. A recession begins when the economy reaches a peak of. Have they the relationship between economic indicators and crime rates in terms of whether there is a correlation between a given indicator and crime? A positive correlation exists when increases in one variable are accompanied by increases in another variable. A negative correlation, on the other hand, occurs when increases in one variable are accompanied by decreases in another variable.

One important concept is the idea that correlation does not imply causation; the presence of two sets of data (two variables) showing similar trends does not indicate that changes in one variable cause any visible changes in the other. Instead, a correlation shows that changes in one variable can, to some extent, predict changes in another variable. For instance, while some neighborhoods may exhibit a relationship between certain types of crime and the economy, other neighborhoods may exhibit a relationship between different types of crime and the economy or may not exhibit a relationship at all.

Consequently, researchers tend to use individual economic indicators, such as the unemployment rate, as a proxy for the state of the economy. However, any given indicator may not be generalizable to the state of the economy as a whole during any one given recession or across recessions.Despite the limitations in using specific economic variables as proxies for a complex economic state, this methodology does allow researchers to isolate variables and analyze their individual.Generalizability is

typically defined as the extent to which the results generated by a variable being studied can be applied to other settings, times, or groups of subjects and be expected to deliver a similar outcome. Specifically, during the most recent economic downturn, many referred to the
unemployment rate and the proportion of home foreclosures as proxies for economic health.

- What are the real factors cause the changes in the crime rates?

Impact of Unemployment on Crime
the unemployment rate is one of the most widely referenced economic indicators. In discussions of potential impacts of the economy on crime rates, many scholars and policy makers use the unemployment rate as a proxy for economic strength. Congress has shown interest in the relationship between the economy—unemployment, in particular—and crime rates since the 1970s. The most recent recession, which was accompanied by a rise in the unemployment rate, once again focused attention on the relationship between unemployment and crime rates.

Researchers and scholars have several theories concerning the relationship between unemployment and crime. One of these theories, the economic theory of crime, assumes that people make rational choices between legitimate activities and criminal activities as a source of economic gain. More specifically, the comparison is between the economic benefit of legitimate work versus that of violent or property crime, after accounting for crime-related costs such as incarceration. Although the theory was originally formulated with an application to all crimes, many researchers have used it in discussions of unemployment and property crime. This theory predicts a positive correlation between unemployment and property crime; in other words, that increases in the unemployment rate will be correlated with increases in property crime rates. The reason for this positive correlation, according to the economic model, is that during periods when there are fewer opportunities for legitimate income, people may turn to illegal activities, while when more jobs are available, the risks of committing a crime may be weighed against the opportunity for legitimate work.

Were a direct link between unemployment and the property crime rate, varying one would necessarily vary the other? The lack of conclusive evidence for a strong, or even significant,correlation between the two suggests that the unemployment rate may have an indirect relationship with the property crime rate. Although unemployment is correlated with overall economic conditions, it may not fully capture other key economic indicators such as work hours, employment stability, and wages. Some researchers, for example, have found that employment stability and wages may correlate more strongly with the property crime rate than does unemployment.

Economic Theories of Crime

What is economic theories of crime ?This brief literature review highlights three key economic frameworks that can be used to explain a persistent social problem in modern society, crime and delinquency: the rational model, the present-oriented or myopic model, and the radical political economic model. Based on a cost-benefit analysis, an individuals decision to engage in crime in the rational model is consistent in the short-and long-term. Present-oriented individuals, however, focus on the short-term benefits without particular concern for the long-term consequences of their actions. The radical political economic model focuses on the following key political and socio-economic factors that sustain crime: relative deprivation, poverty and inequality, unemployment, and class conflict.The conclusion includes a conceptual map integrating the three frameworks.

Some economists and crime psychologists believe that crime is not limited to certain areas or to certain socioeconomic classes
of society. Criminal activities take many forms, including theft, homicide,assault, fraud, embezzlement, and blackmail. So why does crime persist? Are there underlying factors that can explain criminal behavior? Can we lower the incentives for criminal behavior? Do criminals take opportunity costs of committing a crime into account? The social science field has long been interested in these questions.

This literature review focuses on the discipline of economics and its assumptions about individual decisions to commit crime. The standard assumption is that individuals who commit crimes are rational decision makers who expect to gain something from criminal activity, and this gain is greater than the expected costs associated with being caught. Most of the research in this area focuses on the effects of incentives to engage in criminal behavior and on the use of cost-benefit analysis to assess alternative policies to reduce crime. However, not all crime can be categorized as rational behavior. Socioeconomic factors are also assumed to affect crime, and alternative theories to explain criminal activities are used to challenge
the standard assumption of rational behavior. The main objective of this review is to identify the key economic frameworks that are used to explain crime and delinquency. The three key frameworks include the

rational model of crime, the present-oriented or myopic model of crime, and the radical political economic model of crime.

Economists have begun to question whether the standard assumption of rational behavior holds when consideringwhy individuals engage in criminal activity. Can we really assume that all criminals make rational decisions to commit a crime? Individual preferences, psychic factors, and other motivations for crime may play an equally large role in explaining crime. However these factors are much harder to incorporate into economic models of crime. Hence, there is limited empirical research in this area. It will be interesting to see how the growing field of behavioral economics can help to explain crime and delinquency.

The three main economic models of crime are the rationa lmodel, the present oriented or myopic model, and the radical political economic model. Each model emphasizes different factors that influence individual decisions to commit crime and different ways of combating crime. What is the Rational Model of Crime mean?

Economics can be defined as a discipline that studies how scarce resources are allocated by the forces of supply and demand to meet different needs in society. In the same way, economists argue that crime is a result of individuals' making choices between using their scarce resources of time and effort in legitimate or in illegitimate activities. A key assumption is that

when making these choices, individuals are rational and choose the best option based on the available information and resources. Individuals are perceived to be promoting their self-interest by rationally selecting options that provide them with the greatest benefits that are expected to exceed the costs associated with these options.

The profit from crime is traditionally measured in terms of monetary benefits but can also include physical, psychic, and other benefits. The "punishment" or costs of crime include the risk of detection, apprehension, and conviction and the severity of punishment. Economists do not refute that environmental, psychological, and biological factors may affect criminal activity. Nevertheless, they argue that individuals are free to choose between different courses of options available to them. Therefore, as long as there is a rational element of choice available, individuals who decide to commit a crime will react to changes in the probability of apprehension and the severity of punishment .This framework leads to a key concept, namely, the "opportunity cost" of crime. Any decision that involves a choice between two or more options has an opportunity cost. An opportunity cost can be defined as the value of the next best alternative within the context of making a decision. Put differently, an opportunity cost can be viewed as the benefits an individual could have received by taking an alternative decision or action. In essence, the true cost of crime for a potential criminal is the opportunity cost of spending time in prison. The opportunity cost varies among individuals irrespective of the length of incarceration.

The rational framework distinguishes between static and dynamic models of crime. In a static model, individuals compare the costs and benefits of engaging in crime in a single time period. In a dynamic model, the individual considers multiple time periods. Decisions made in the past, for example, impact the decision-making process in the present.

- Is Unemployment caused crime by poor macro economy environment factor?

Different models examine the different relationships between unemployment and crime. Some economic models assume that unemployment either lowers the opportunity costs of crime or that it increases the need to supplement income from sources other than legal employment. However, how do individuals form expectations about their earnings potential in the labor market? If there is a considerable gap between what the individual believes is attainable (group experience) and what is unattainable (larger society experience), an individual perceives this gap as relative deprivation. Hence the opportunity costs of crime may be reduced because the returns from regular employment are seen as minimal. In contrast, if the larger society also suffers from unemployment, the shortage of employment opportunities may still be considered equitable. attention that crimes, such as burglary or theft, receive in comparison with white collar crime, although the latter type of crimes represent a larger proportion of monetary losses than the former type.

Crime accompanies social life from its very beginning – it occurs in every society and in every stage of its development, regardless of its structure, system or historical period. Undoubtedly, crime is a consequence of many social and economic problems which constantly change, therefore there are so many controversial and unresolved issued connected with the influence of social and economical factors on crime. This article is an attempt to find an answer to whether the socio-economic factors clearly have a substantial impact on crime.

Regardless of whether we like it or not – crime is a constant component of our life. The crime level is

influenced by lots of factors
which nature is heterogeneous. Among them, we may distinguish the socio - economic situation of the offender. Statistics (not only Polish) seem to confirm the assumption that there is a strong connection between social and economic conditions and the level of crime .

- SOCIO - ECONOMIC FACTORS CAUSES CRIME RATE INCREASES

Crime and changes in the structure of crime are both affected by such elements as: the degree of economic development, socio - political system that functions in a given country, the progress of industrialization and urbanization, transformations in social structure which are age-related to members of the society and finally, migrations. Transformations may be carried out in a revolutionary way or throughout a longer period of time, they can also occur suddenly as a result of some turbulent changeovers and rapid changes which happen in a given community.

In the case of our country one should consider political changes, accompanied by destabilizing and disintegrative processes, political changes with the transition from a communist to a democratic regime. Further modifications were related to the economic system, changes in ownership structure and the emergence of structural unemployment .New conditions caused a shift in social structure, namely, new social groups were
formed, social hierarchy was changed, and many social groups suffered economic degradation.

- The influence of socio - economic factors on crime

Therefore, one should ask a question whether in fact the economic situation shapes the level of crime rate . While being under constant modifications and transformations, society will never stay unchanged. Changes in the number, gender, age structure, migration (demographic changes) also have their mutual influence related to the economy, system of power, education, health protection, religion, and crime. Poor economic situation may translate into crime by an increase in unemployment. It should be noted that unemployment, naturally connected with the economy may have a different dimension. We distinguish between the structural, cyclical, long-term, and frictional unemployment. Because of the social and demographic factors, such as gender, age or education level of people affected by the unemployment, there may be various relationships and impact on criminal activity.An analysis of police statistics shows that the highest intensity of crime occurs among unemployed people who are under thirty years of age . If an individual is affected by long-term unemployment, he or she starts to be affected by the consequences of such a situation, namely a sense of exclusion, injustice, and finally the lack of hope of finding a legitimate source of income . The analysis shows that unemployment brings on crime against property rather than violence . However, it should be noted that the increase in unemployment in various ways may affect particular social groups by increasing or decreasing their criminal activity. At this point one should outline four specific relationships between unemployment and crime as below:

· Some offenders combine their legal professional work with criminal activity. Legal business is treated as a camouflage for illegal operation. In this case, the development of unemployment may reduce the "gray zone" business, as the legal work, in this case, gives a sense of security for conducting criminal activity.

· There is a number of crimes, possible to be committed only during conducting activities while being legally employed, for example: "handing over bribes to officials", "employee theft". In those situations the growth of unemployment will inhibit the number of crimes of the above mentioned type, rather than increase them.

· Young people, in particular distinguish between two options: being legally employed, or being involved in a criminal activity. If the lack of work prevails, the willingness to take an income from illegal sources may be decisive. Unemployment, in this perspective may cause an increase in crime.

· There are people for whom unemployment is strictly related to their living style. This group of people treat legal work as an abnormal situation – those people are not part of the labor market. For them, the lack of employment is part of their cultural identity, and criminal activity is, in their environment, a socially accepted source of income. In this case, an increase in unemployment will have no influence on the formation of criminal behavior.

Further analysis of inter-relations of factors related to the discussed problem may incline to believe that in a period of an economic recession, a higher level of crime against property and lower against the person is being observed, whereas, during a period of prosperity (an economic boom) the situation is

other way round: higher level of crime against the person and lower against property is being distinguished. Apart from unemployment other economic factors such as: poverty, the level, dynamics and diversity of earnings and the pace of economic development influence the crime rate. Poverty has long been the factor which has been strongly associated with criminal activity. As it was indicated by Alain Peyrefitte, "crime is the child of poverty".

While trying to explain the influence of socio - economic changes on crime, a number of changes in the economic system should be taken into account, such as the emergence of
economic crises, periods of economic prosperity, the processes of European unification, EU enlargement, globalization, the processes of industrialization and urbanization. If the economic components affect almost all types of social activity, there must be a link between them and the crime. Conditions, economic tension may create some situations, often stressful situations that may facilitate criminal activity . Initially, the analysis of the relationship between social and economic transformation and changes in the crime indicated that there is a causal connection, but now this assumption is not so obvious. One may only unquestionably
talk about correlation between a group of various factors, also non-economical and certain types of crime. A good economic situation, a period of prosperity may both influence either increase or decrease in the number of offenses.

First of all, it may increase the possibility to commit a crime as the easiness and availability of products make them an easy target for a thief or even a person who has a desire to steal an item without really the need to have it. Abundance of goods cause that products may become an object of a crime (e.g become vandalized). Furthermore, if people have too much leisure, they tend to change their lifestyle – and this change is associated with taking part in or participate in events or actions with other people. This

causes a greater opportunity for people to be involved in a prohibited
actions and crimes against the person. A period of prosperity may, on the other hand decrease the possibility to commit a crime as people stick to generally accepted social standards and the desire to commit an illegal actions e.g. theft, swindle is reduced. They feel more socially secured and safe. The better social and economic status people have, the lower need to be involved in something prohibited by law. In case of a well-paid job, also motivational elements appear as well as the fear of the consequences of a wrongful act. In literature of this field, there is no evidence that there is a connection between the level of crime and the level of industrialization. However, there is a strong connection between the level of crime and spatial mobility of the population, and the size of migration.

The internationalization of crime causes intensification of organized crime. Possibilities to commit a crime also change – smuggling, tax frauds, economic crime, production of drugs and weapon, money frauds, prostitution, ?money laundering", customs offenses, corruption. The changing structure of crime, its forms and ways of committing it indicate a real change in social structure and transformations of the social life as well as missing norms and values of societies which in a given historical period may be observed.

In conclusion,the discussed and analyzed socio - economic factors incline to believe that social and economical sphere of human life is interrelated and interdependent. There are certain correlations with the crime level and social behavior as well as with economy and human vulnerability to commit an offense. However, careful The influence of socio - economic factors on crime examination in this respect is still needed. Causal dependencies which occur in societies on every stage of their development are difficult to explain.So how to carry out on the research, analysis of recovery plans and criminal statistics as well as literature allowed to form a conclusion that people should not only focus on individuals in crime prevention programs but on such forms of activity that would be targeted to whole societies. Preventive measures should aim at reducing both economic and social inequalities, e.g balance the level of income or promote social cohesion. Although various crime preventive strategies and programs continue to be developed , they may only reduce crime rate on a small scale, basically they will not have a clear influence on the increase or decrease in a criminal activity in a particular country or in a global dimension as too many social and economic factors should be taken into account.

Is poor macro economic environment a main root to crime causation ?

Is poor macro economic environment cause crime essentially? Economic Theories indicate the roots of crime are diverse and a discipline like economics, predicated on rational behavior, may be at something of a disadvantage in explaining a phenomenon largely viewed as irrational. A recent survey suggests that three general issues are of central concern in the economics of crime literature: the effects of incentives on criminal behavior, how decisions interact in a market-setting, and the use of cost-benefit analysis to assess alternative policies to reduce crime will focus on the role of incentives on criminal behavior.

However, trend in criminal participation rates in most industrialized economies is a difficult task. Many social scientists argue that crime is closely related to work,

education and poverty and that truancy, youth unemployment and crime are by products or even measures of social exclusion. "Blue-collar"criminals often have limited education and possess limited labor market skills. These characteristics partly explain the poor employment records and low legitimate earnings of most criminals. These sort of issues originally led economists to examine the relationship between wages and unemployment rates on crime. More recently economists have also considered the benefits and costs of educational programs to
reduce crime.

A related question concerns the impact of sanctions. For example, does increased imprisonment lower the crime rate? How does the deterrent effect of formal sanctions arise? Although criminologists have been tackling such issues for many years, it is only recently that economists have entered the arena of controversy. This is not surprising given the high levels of crime and the associated allocation of public and private resources towards crime prevention. The expenditure on the criminal justice system (police, prisons, prosecution/defense and courts) is a significant proportion of government budgets. In addition, firms and households are spending increasingly more on private security.

The incentive-based economic model of crime is a model of decision making in risky situations.

Economists analyse the way in which individual attitudes toward risk affect the extent of illegal behavior. In most of the early literature, the economic models of crime are single-period individual choice models. These models generally see the individual as deciding to allocate time with criminal activity as one possible use of time. A key feature is the notion of utility; judgements are made of the likely gain to be realised (the 'expected utility') from a particular choice of action. Individuals are assumed to be rational decision-makers who engage in either legal or illegal activities according to the expected utility from each activity. An individual's participation in illegal activity is, therefore, explained by the opportunity cost of illegal activity (for example, earnings from legitimate work), factors that influence the returns to illegal activity (for example, detection and the severity of punishment), and by tastes and preferences for illegal activity.

Economists see criminal activity as being similar to paid employment in that it requires time and produces an income. Clearly, the dichotomy between either criminal activity or legal activity is an oversimplification. For example, individuals could engage in criminal activities while employed since they have greater opportunities to commit crime; similarly, some criminals may jointly supplement work income with crime income in order to satisfy their needs. A secondary problem with the economist's choice model, which was highlighted in our opening comments, is that young people are more likely to participate in crime long before they participate in the labor market. This observation raises questions about the appropriateness of the economic model of crime in explaining juvenile crime.

Economic models of criminal behavior have focused on sanction effects (e.g. deterrence issue) and the relationship between work and crime. In the main, these models have not directly addressed the role of education in offending. It could be argued that unemployment is the conduit through which other factors influence the crime rate. For example, poor educational attainment may be highly correlated with the incidence of crime. However, this may also be a key determinant of unemployment. Although educational variables have been included as covariates with crime rates, they have not received a great deal of attention in correlational studies.

To the basic theory ,economic Model of Criminal Behavior: Basic theory is as mentioned in the overview, the economic model of crime is a standard model of decision making where individuals choose between criminal activity and legal activity on the basis of the expected utility from those acts. It is assumed that participation in criminal activity is the result of an optimizing individual responding to incentives. Among the factors that influence an individual's decision to engage in criminal activities are (i) the expected gains from crime relative to earnings from legal work (ii) the chance (risk) of being caught and convicted, (iii) the extent of punishment and (iv) the opportunities in legal activities. Specifying an equation to capture the incentives in the criminal decision is a natural first step in most analyses of the crime as work models. The most important of these gives the relative rewards of legal and illegal activity. For example, the economic model sees the criminal as committing a crime if the expected gain from criminal activity exceeds the gain from
legal activity, generally work.

Just as in benefit-cost analysis, when comparing alternative strategies, interest centers on the returns from one decision vis-a-vis returns from another decision. For example, a preference for crime over work implies the earnings gap between legal
and illegal activities must rise when the probability of being caught and the severity of punishment increases. Attitudes

towards risk are central to economic models of criminal choice. For example, if the individual is said to dislike risk (i.e., to be risk averse) then he will respond more to changes in the chances of being apprehended than to changes in the extent of punishment, other things being equal. Becker developed a comparative-static model that considered primarily the deterrent effect of the criminal justice system. As we will see, how individuals respond to deterrent and incapacitation effects of sanctions has generated considerable theoretical and empirical interest from economists.

Thus, severe sentencing and improvements in legal work opportunities of criminals must be expected jointly to reduce crime. Of course, this assumes that crime and work are determined by the same factors and that higher legitimate earnings increase the probability of working. In the early literature, economists applied static one period time allocation models to analyse criminal behavior. In other words, crime and work are assumed to be substitute activities; if an individual allocates more time to work, he will commit less crime because he will have less time to do so. The basic economic model of crime is static or comparative static in economic jargon because it does not see the potential criminal as considering more than a single time period when making his decision.

Early studies of criminal behavior by economists can be criticized for being set in a static framework. Economic models of crime are typically estimated as staticmodels, though there are many reasons to suspect dynamic effects matter, both theoretically through habit formation, interdependence of preferences, capital accumulation, addiction, peer group effects, etc., and empirically through improvements in fit when lagged dependent variables or autocorrelated residuals are included in the model. Labor economists have long been interested in state dependence, the fact that activities chosen in the current period may be strongly affected by the individual's activities in the previous period.

Flinn incorporates human capital formation in a time-allocation model. In his model, human capital is accumulated at work, not at school. Consequently, crime takes time away from work and hence diminishes the amount of human capital

accumulated. The diminished human capital leads to lower future wages and hence less time spent working. Since crime and work are substitutes in his model, the decline in time allocated to work leads to increased participation in criminal activities.

In nowadays global labor market, the basic idea underlying the model is that young men have two types of jobs available to

them –skilled and unskilled – where wage profiles are rising in the former (due to accumulation of human capital, training and experience) and flat in the latter (no training). If discounted wages are equalized across jobs, the unskilled wage would start above and end below skilled wage. Also, human capital theory suggests that job

stability will be greater in skilled sector than in the unskilled sector. Given these predictions, and assuming that a criminal conviction adversely affects prospects of getting a skilled job, it is likely that conviction is associated with higher pay and higher job instability. So, low skillful workers usually do criminal behaviors more than high skillful workers in our societies nowadays.

Concerning how to examine the impact of legitimate labor market experiences (e.g., unemployment) and sanctions on criminal behavior whether they have relationship question? Broadly speaking, the empirical findings are that (i) poor legitimate labor market opportunities of potential criminals, such as low wages and high rates of unemployment, increases the supply of criminal activities and (ii) sanctions deter crime. Unemployment could be taken to influence the opportunity cost of illegal activity. High rates of unemployment growth could be taken to imply a restriction on the availability of legal activities, and thus serve to ultimately reduce the opportunity cost of engaging in illegal activities. Although theoretically well-defined, most empirical studies of the unemployment-crime relationship have provided mixed
evidence. Instead of primarily focusing on crime as a function of unemployment, they use a richer set of controls, like deterrence, employment status, age, education, race and neighbourhood
characteristics.

One problem with most work and crime models is that they assume both activities are mutually exclusive. This may be a problematic assumption when considering disadvantaged youths. The fact that a youth can shift from crime to an unskilled job and back again or can commit crime while holding a legal job means that the supply of youths to crime will be quite elastic with respect to relative rewards from crime vis-a-vis legal work or to the number of criminal opportunities. From the 1970s through the 1990s the labor market prospects for unskilled workers in most

OECD countries has deteriorated considerably. In particular, the real earnings of young unskilled men fell, while income inequality rose. This suggests that as the earnings gap widens, relative deprivation increases, which in turn leads to increases in crime.

A substantial problem that has been ignored in the vast majority of empirical studies is nonstationarity of crime rates. A time-series is said to be nonstationary if (1) the mean and/or variance does not remain constant over time and (2) covariance between observations depends on the time at which they occur. In the US, the index crime rate appears strongly nonstationary, for the most part being integrated of order one with both deterministic and stochastic trends (a random variable whose mean value and variance are time-dependent is said to follow a stochastic trend) .The empirical results suggest a long-run equilibrium relationship between crime, prison population, female labor supply and durable consumption.

The explanatory variables include the number of juveniles or adults in custody per crime; the number of juveniles or adults in custody per juvenile or adult; economic variables, including the state unemployment rate and demographic variables, including race and legal drinking age, and dummy variables for year and state. Levitt finds that juvenile crime is negatively related to the severity of penalties, and that juvenile offenders are at least as responsive to sanctions as adults. Interestingly, he finds that the difference between the punishments given to youths and adults helps explain sharp changes in crimes committed by youths as they reach the age of majority.

Most economic work on crime has focused on the deterrent effect of the criminal justice system and on the interrelationship between work and crime. Empirical work provides some, but not unambiguous support for the deterrence hypothesis. Recent work by economist suggest that the relationship between work and crime may be far more complicated than implied by economic models.

The rise in juvenile crime rates has focused increasing attention on youth crime. This has forced economists to expand their thinking to incorporate such things as education, peer group effects and the influence of family and community. Increasingly both theoretical and empirical work on the economics of crime has come to use dynamic models. Theoretical work is developing multi-period models of crime. Empirically economists are using both panel data techniques and modern time series techniques to examine the dynamics of criminal behavior.

● CRIMINOLOGICAL THEORIES ABOUT

why people commit crime are used—and misused, if poor global economic environment factor was main factor causes people do criminal behaviors?

Every day by legislative policy makers and community corrections managers when they develop new initiatives, sanctions, an programs; and these theories are also being applied—and misapplied—by line community corrections officers in the workplace as they classify, supervise, counsel, and control offenders placed on their caseloads. The purpose of this article is to provide a brief overview of the major theories of crime causation and then to consider the implications of these criminological theories for current and future community corrections practice. Four distinct groups of theories will be examined: classical theories, biological theories, psychological theories, and sociological theories of crime causation.

While the
assumptions of classical criminology have been used to justify a wide range of sentencing and corrections policies and practices over the past several decades, it is also possible to identify the influence of other theories of crime causation on corrections policies and practices during this same period.

As we examine each group of theories, we consider how—and why—the basic functions of probation and parole officers change based on the theory of crime causation under review.
When considering the link between theory and practice, it is important to remember the following basic truth: Criminologists disagree about both the causes and solutions to our crime problem. This does not mean that criminologists have little to offer to probation and parole officers in terms of practical advice; to other community corrections programs are to the contrary, we think a discussion of "cause" is be successful as "people changing" agencies. Critical to the ongoing debate over the appro-But can we reasonably expect such diversity priate use of community-based sanctions, and flexibility from community corrections and the development of effective community agencies, or is it more likely that one theory—corrections policies, practices, and programs. or group of theories—will be the dominant.

However, the degree of uncertainty on the influence on community corrections practice?
cause—or causes—of our crime problem in Based on recent reviews of United States academic community suggests that a rections history, we suspect that one group of
certain degree of skepticism is certainly in theories—supported by a dominant political order when

"new" crime control strategies are ideology—will continue to dominate until introduced. We need to look carefully at the the challenges to its efficacy move the field—
theory of crime causation on which these new both ideologically and theoretically—in a new initiatives are based. It is our view that since direction. We may—or may not—be at such a each group of theories we describe is appli- watershed point in the United States today.

An Overview of Criminological Theories

Classically-based criminologists explain criminal behavior as a conscious choice by individuals based on an assessment of the costs and benefits of various forms of criminal activity. Biologically-based criminologists explain criminal behavior as determined—in part—by the presence of certain inherited traits that may increase the likelihood of criminal behavior.

Psychologically-based criminologists explain criminal behavior as the consequence of individual factors, such as negative early childhood experiences and inadequate socialization, that result in criminal thinking patterns and/or incomplete cognitive development.

Sociologically-based criminologists explain criminal behavior as primarily influenced by a variety of community-level factors that appear to be related—both directly and indirectly—to
the high level of crime in some of our (often poorest) communities, including blocked legitimate opportunity, the existence of subcultural values that support criminal behavior, a breakdown of community-level informal social controls, and an unjust system of criminal laws and criminal justice.

To a classical criminologist, the answer is
simple: The benefits of law breaking (such as money,

property, revenge, and status) simply outweigh the potential costs/consequences of getting caught and convicted. When viewed

from a classical perspective, we are all capable of committing crime in a given situation, but we make a rational decision (to act or desist) based on our analysis of the costs and benefits of the action. If this is true, then it is certainly possible to deter a potential offender by (1) developing a system of "sentencing" in which the punishment outweighs the (benefit of the) crime, and (2) ensuring both punishment certainty and celerity through efficient police

and court administration. "Classical" theories of criminal behavior are appealing to criminal justice policy makers, because they are based

on the premise that the key to solving the crime problem is to have a strong system of formal social control. In other words, the classical theorist believes that the system can make a difference, regardless of the myriad of individual and social ills that exist. During the past four decades, a number of federal, state, and local programs have been initiated to improve the deterrent capacity of the criminal justice system, including proactive police strategies to ensure greater certainty of apprehension,priority prosecution/speedy trial strategies to ensure greater celerity (speed) in the court process, and determinate/ mandatory sentencing strategies to ensure greater punishment certainty and severity.

To further our deterrent aims, we have significantly increased our institutional capacity during this same period and passed legislation that includes mandatory minimum periods of incarceration for drug-related crimes, while simultaneously developing a series of surveillance-oriented intermediate sanctions (e.g., intensive probation supervision, electronic monitoring/house arrest) for a subgroup of the offenders under community supervision.

It is apparent from these initiatives that classical assumptions about crime causation are still being used as the basis for current crime control strategies. Some have argued that our four-decade-long emphasis on "deterrencebased"crime control policies has resulted in safer communities; in fact, by most standard measures (crime rates, victimization rates) we have less crime and less violence today than at any point since the early 1970s.

With most experts estimating that about a quarter of the crime decline can be linked to tougher sentencing policies, while

three quarters of the decline have been attributed to other factors (such as the economy, education, and immigration). A careful review of the evaluation research indicates that community-based sanctions does not support the notion that increased surveillance and control reduces recidivism (that is, an offender's likelihood of rearrest, reconviction, and/ or re-incarceration). There are two possible explanations for these findings: (1) the underlying assumptions of classical criminologists (i.e., most people are rational, and weigh the costs and benefits of various acts in the same manner) are wrong (e.g., people commit crimes for emotional reasons, because of mental illness, and/or because they believe the criminal act is justified, given circumstances and prevailing community values); or (2) the current sentencing strategies and community corrections programs need to be even tougher and deterrence-oriented (in other words, the theory is correct; it just has not been implemented correctly).

While community corrections populations and probation rates also remain high, and continue to use multiple conditions
that emphasize surveillance and control (through drug testing, electronic monitoring, curfews, and now social media monitoring).
For example, in the name of deterrence, legislation has been passed in several states allowing the lifetime supervision of paroled.

The final group of psychological theories
focuses on the potential link between personality and criminality. Although there is currently much debate on whether personality
characteristics play a significant role in determining subsequent criminal behavior, a number of prominent criminologists have
argued that "the root causes of crime are not...social issues [high unemployment, bad schools] but deeply ingrained features of the
human personality and its early experiences. Low intelligence, an impulsive personality, and a lack of empathy for other people are
among the leading individual characteristics
of people at risk for becoming offenders".

- THE IMPACT OF CRIMINOLOGICAL THEORY WHETHER POOR ECONOMIC ENVIRONMENT IS THE REAL REASON TO INFLUENCE CRIME RATE RAISES

This question concerns to how to implement and the development of strategies to assess community "risk" and then relocate offenders who currently reside in "high-risk" neighborhoods to lower-risk areas, utilizing the lure of new job opportunities or housing incentives. A final group of sociological theories of crime causation can be identified, based on the premise that people become criminals not because of some inherent characteristic, personality defect, or other sociologically-based "pressure" or influence, but because of decisions made by those in positions of power in government, especially those in the criminal justice system. The social strategies implementation to reduce crime rate increases may include as below:

Intervention Strategy

(1) Strategies emphasize education, skill development,and employment opportunity.

(2) Strategies emphasize community-level value change, alternatives to gang involvement, and offender relocation.

(3) Strategies target improving community structural conditions, resource availability, and collective efficacy; strengthening informal community social control mechanisms; and eliminating poverty pockets.

(4) Strategies focus on the breakdown of informal social control mechanisms— attachment, commitment, involvement, and belief—and emphasize the importance of the relationship between the offender and his/her probation/parole officer.

(5) Strategies designed to target the turning points in the lifecourse

that have been directly related to desistance among adult offenders—marriage, employment, military service,

and offender relocation.

(6) Strategies focus on the use of alternative dispute/ conflict resolution strategies that result in lower levels of formal criminal justice system involvement in the lives of community residents; and on the application of community/ restorative justice principles in traditional

criminal justice settings, including community corrections.

All these strategies are supposed that the country's crime rate raises is not due to poor economic environment factor influence mainly. The country's crime rate raising is based on other non economic related factors influence.

Given the potential negative consequences of labeling,we need to ask ourselves: (1) which laws do we really need to enforce? and (2) which offenders can (and should) we divert from the formal court process?

A number of observers have suggested probation and parole officers do not have an adequate "professional base" to do the job we ask them to do. However, it is our view that it is impossible to assess the qualifications of community corrections personnel unless we first clearly define the primary job orientation of the community corrections officer: Do we want our line staff to emphasize treatment or control? As we have indicated throughout this article, how we answer the "why" (or causation) question (Why did the offender commit this crime?) will determine not only our general orientation toward certain categories of crime (e.g., drug offenses, violent crime) and groups of offenders (e.g., sex offenders, gang members, drunk drivers), but also the types of functions we will expect community corrections to perform.

A number of line probation and parole officers only have an undergraduate degree, while some have even less formal

education. This diversity in educational background would be a cause for concern if we could clearly establish a relationship between education and the job itself. Unfortunately, we do not have a firm grasp on the types of skills necessary to be an effective probation or parole officer in the next decade. While a number of “get tough” intermediate sanctions programs have been developed based on classical assumptions about crime control (e.g., intensive supervision, house arrest, boot camps), these programs still include only a small percentage (approximately 10 percent) of all offenders under community supervision. If these programs continue to expand, it appears that we will need to draw our POs from the pool of undergraduate criminal justice majors, perhaps requiring some prior experience as a police officer or corrections guard. Such “deskilling” is an inevitable consequence of the movement away from treatment and toward the technology of control.

I shall indicate the developing country, India case example to explain why and how poor economic environment can impact crime rate to be raised in possible as below:

The Economist (2018, pp.7-16) indicated that India Women unemployment rate raised that it had relationship between India poor economic environment and India itself country’s unemployment women. It explain as below:

India labour force, women have been falling away at an alarming pace. The female employment rate in India, counting both the formal and informal economy, has raised from an already-low 35% in 2005 to just 26% now. IN that time the economy has more than doubled in size and the number of working-age women has grown by a quarter, to 470 million. Yetnearly 10m fewer womwn are in jobs. A rise in female employment rates to the male level would provide India with an extra 235 m workers, more than the

EU has of either geneder,and more than enough to fill all the factories in the rest in Asia. India has high young female unemnployed number, it may due to many girls need to leave schools to find jobs to do because their families are poor.

However, Economist also indicated other problmes in India nowadays, they include that lacking of employment opportunities.

The workforce has shifted from jobs more often done by women , especially farming, where most Indian women work but are being displaced by mechanisation. At the same time, inflexible and unreformed labour markets have hampered the rise of manufacturing and low-level services, the gateway for women in other poor countries. IN neighhouring Bangladesh, whose customs are not so different from India's. a boom in gament manufacturing has increased the number of working women by 50% since 2005. In Vietnam three-quarters of women work. But the mega-factories that boosted female employment there are largely absent in India.

So, it seems that India's manufacturing industry can not develop successfully, it may due to it lacks confidnece to let overseas or domestic investors to develop any kinds of manufacturing businesses in India as well as India lacks high technological skillful workers number is shortage to supply to India's manufacturing industries in

India's labor market. SO, it explains that India's poor economy and low technological manufacturing industry development

and high India female unemployment number, they can bring India's crime rate to be raised in possible.

In fact, India has many male workers who have been encountering unemployment for a long time, instead of India has many young females can not find any jobs to work in India easily. When India has been still encountering the challenge of lacking of enough manufacturing jobs to supply to them to do, instead of farming jobs, this primary industry jobs, e.g. farmers, fruit pickers , cow feeding etc. farming jobs. It can not solve India unemployment challenge. Because some India high educational young people had graduated in university, but they still feel difficulties to find any suitable jobs to do, it may due to there are less overseas and domestic investors have confidence to set up their businesses in India. SO, high educational jobs are shortage in India.Then, it causes India's economic environment will be become more worse to compare past. So, it seems that India's worse economic enviroment will influence

unemploment rises and crime rate rises. I believe that they have direct relationship betweem them.

India's worse economic environment also causes many employees have no preferred the stability of permanent employment mind, they only choose contracted employment or short term , temporary employment in India. They only earn hour paid , or day paid and they feel difficulties to earn monthly paid in India labor market easily.

For India Mc Donald's jobs example, a America fast food company has taken things the furthest, outsourcing 100% of its restaurant

jobs, Servers, cooks and cleaners at India McDonald's are no longer employees of the firm or its franchisees, but bid for positions at the till on an hourly basis thtough TaskRabbit, an online labour platform.So, most functions were completed in-house by permanent, full time employees. Many people worked for only one or two employers during their careers. That arrangement had been changed by a unreasonable business logic.

It implies that some overseas big company , such as America Mc Donald restaurant also can not provide reasonable welfare to India workers, then they will feel hopeless to earn reasonable wage treatment when they believe that they can work in any one overseas large organizations. In long term, Indian will feel long term unemployment feeling, although, they still have fill time jobs to do because many full time jobs are contract, short term, temporary. So, they need to often to change new employers, even some Indian people working performance are excellent. If Indian working people are luck, they can change another new employers very easily. Otherwise, if they are unluck, then they need to wait short time, e.g. one month or three months, even, they need to wait longer time, e.g. more than six months or more than one year. So, many Indian working people are feeling sudden unemployment occurrence in possible. When their employment contracts are finished ,even if employers decline their offer contract continue. So, if some Indians working people wait need to spend long time to search any jobs, due to jobs are not enough. They will feel unemployment , then crime rate will be influenced to be raised from long time unemployment factor in possible in India nowadays society.

In conclusion, if some countries feel their crime rate raising reason is not caused by poor economic environment factor, they can attempt to apply above strategies to solve crime rating problems to investigate whether poor economic environment factor is the main factor to influence their crime rate raising in possible.

Reference

The Economist, How India Fails its women, July 7 the 2018. pp. 7-16

● The relationship between welfare economics and crime rate

I believe that whether the country has better or worse welfare
economic environment or its welfare is improved to satisfy its citizen's living of standard, it will bring effect whether its society's
crime rate is more less. I shall explain why and
how the country welfare will influence its crime rate to be increased or decreased as below reasons:

What does the new welfare economics mean? It can be explained that how the county citizens interpersonal comparison of utility and social welfare function to their country's welfare policy to let they feel more satisfactory or less satisfactory. Their satisfaction can include leisure and non-leisure consumption satisfaction daily. So, if the country can give more welfares to let its citizen to feel more satisfaction on leisure and consumption aspects. Then, they won't choose to do any crime activities more easily.

In fact, economists have used no methods of scientific research in arriving at their conclusions about whether the country can provide better or worse economic welfare, which can influence the society's crime rate is raised or decreased. However, I shall attempt to explain that why any country's welfare can let its citizen to satisfy more or less, then it can influence the country's crime rate to be increased or decreased.

Every country's economic welfare was said to be a part of total welfare, as well as it can be brought directly or indirectly into relation with money. Why do some countries change their social welfare, then their crime rate can be improved to reduce really? In other words, a less satisfaction to a man with more money than it will to one with less money. Based on this assumption, when the country has good welfare to provide the low income people, then they will feel more satisfaction on their daily living needs. They won't feel worry their basic foods, living needs. Consequently, the society will increase many low income people , they won't feel difficulty to live, then stealing , fighting etc. opposed social crime behaviors or activities will ought to be decreased, due to the low income people feel or believe their country can feel what they have real essential needs at the moment. The low income people can feel safe to live in the country. Then, the country's crime rate ought to be decreased. So, it seems that crime rate increases or decreases, it has relationship between the country's welfare satisfaction to their essential needs, in specially the low income group.

Why does poor welfare influence the low Income people do crime behaviors more easily? It is simple, for example, when two consumers , they enter the supermarket to make choice to buy apples to eat. When the high income consumer performs to take any good taste apples to buy to eat. The another low income consumer or unemployed consumer , he looks the another consumer is taking any good taste apples to choose which one is the best apple to buy. During their apply choice process, the low income Or unemployed apple consumer will feel unhappy when he knows the another consumer had chosen the most good taste apples to buy to eat in the supermarket. However, due to the country can not provide the better welfare to support the low income or poor person or unemployed person has enough money to buy any good taste apples to eat in the supermarket. Then, the lacking enough social welfare person , he will do stealing apples crime behavior in the supermarket more easily if he brings one plastic bags. So, if the country has many low income people or poor people or unemployed people are living in the country, they feel that their government can not provide enough welfare to support their essential living need. Then, they will choose to do crime behaviors more easily. Consequently, the country's crime rate will also be raised in possible.

So, I believe that any country's crime rate is more or less, it has relationship to its low income people whether they feel their country government can give more or less welfare to support their basic daily living needs in order to do any crime behavior more easily. Because one individual's happiness is also , to some extent, dependent on what others consume. Obviously, the standard of living or welfare level of his family is not a matter of indifference to a man. But we do not avoid the difficulty by taking family as a unit. So, when the country has many families are living, if there are many families' fathers , they are not employing or they are often working in the low income level as well as they government can not provide enough welfares to support their living need. It will bring that they feel living pressure to support their children to learn and wife's living need, if their wives are housewives role or without job housewives. So, low income or poor families will do crime behaviors more easily to compare single people, because single people do not need to support their wives and children living cost. So, if the country's families householder group number is more than single householder group number, then the country ought concentrate on supporting more welfare to the householder families group living needs to reduce their living pressure, e.g. children education assistance, handicapped assistance, low income short time welfare assistance, wife short time uncmployed assistance or wife low income assistance. When , they feel lesser living pressure from their government's welfare assistance. Then, these low income families won't do any family fighting or violence or killing themselves families crime behaviors more easily in society.

So, when the country can improved its welfare to be better, then it can encourage many low income people have ability to consume. It will bring its business and economic environment to be better. So, it has case and effect relationship between welfare and economic environment and crime rate to any countries. The most realistic general assumption , we can make is that, when a man saves he is normally saving up to buy a collection similar in composition to that which he is buying when he saves. Therefore, when comparing his welfare for, says, two different years, we must , in effect, scale up his expenditure in the one year until it is equal to his income of that year, and then ask whether, in the other year, he could have bought the scaled-up collection of the one year.

So, every country's government needs to arrange the reasonable welfare to give the different living needs people in itself country. It can ask this question in order to evaluate every low income or poor people's real welfare need, the question is : Could the poor or low income person have bought last year's collection of goods? So, the country government can gather every poor or low income welfare need applicants' past year consumption or purchase price, kinds of product information, e.g. the low income or poor welfare assistance applicant whether he had enough income to buy any electric products , e.g. desktop, laptop computer(s), television, wash machine, fan, air condition etc. home electric products for his family to use last year. If the welfare assistance applicant had any last year electric products purchase record, then I believe that he still have enough income to support his family living, because these are not his basic living need. It means that he ought have enough money to support his family living need in this year. In simple, his welfare assistance ought be less amount to other welfare assistance applicants, they had not bought any home electric products for their families to use last year. So, it is one good evaluation method to assess whether government ought give how much welfare assistance to every welfare assistance applicant in our societies nowadays. Instead, how many number of children number to the families, old age parents are living with or without living to their sons or daughters together, how many children , they are studying primary, secondary or university etc. families member living dependence factor will also need to be considered to assess every family welfare assistance needs. However, it is reasonable that when the family has many lacking independent ability of members who are living together, then this family ought be provided more welfare assistance need to compare the family has many independent ability of members who are living together, because when family has many independent members are living together, they must have more income source to compare the family has less independent members are living members are living together. It means that the family total income must be enough to support whose living need more easily to compare the less number independent family member case.

Thus, welfare economics and ethics can not then , be separated. They are inseparable because the welfare is a value terminology. The answer is that it could be such a system was held to be anything, for example, welfare or happiness, it would once again be emotive and ethical. The subject is one about which nothing interesting can be said without value judgements, for the reason that every country government needs take a moral interest in welfare and happiness to let it poor people or low income people feel less living pressure, when they can feel their government is really considerate their living needs. Also if we propose to use a certain criterion for an increase the economic welfare of an individual, then the country ought can raise the poor or low income people's consumption ability or consumption desires. Consequently, when their consumption behaviors are encouraged to raise any kinds of products are sold easily from them. The country's economy will be improved to be better. Then, the stealing crime cases will also cause to be decreased directly.

In conclusion, I believe that these above cases can explain that why it have direct relationship between welfare economy and consumer behavior and crime rate.

Every country government ought considerate how to arrange the reasonable welfare level to satisfy the different real welfare need applicants' real living needs in order to avoid unfair welfare assistance treatment to let every welfare assistance applicant feel unfair and angry to themselves country government. Thus, welfare economy has real relationship to influence every country's consumer behaviors or consumption desires to be increase or decrease as well as their crime behavioral causation.

CHAPTER FOUR

The relationship between educational challenges and social challenges cause

Nowadays, we are facing different kids of social challenges, e.g. some poor countries, e.g. Africa, China, they have many poor families, they can not provide good education to let them to have chance to go to school to learn, even secondary school level or university level. So, these countries have many young people can not enroll to secondary or university to further to learn, instead of primary school, many families have effort to provide themselves children to learn because their government only assist them to pay free school fee for primary students. So, when their children will lose learning chance if their families have not effort to help them to pay secondary or university education. It causes many young people feel difficult to find good jobs to do, due to their education levels are low reason. When they can not find any jobs to do, moreover due to labor market competition is serious, when low level jobs supplying number can not be more than low educational level job seekers to satisfy their finding jobs needs. Consequently, it must bring social challenges. It is due to school feel are high, e.g. secondary and university educational fees may cause many poor families cannot help their next generation to pay high educational fees to continue to finish their secondary or university education.

Hence, when the country has many families are low income, it will bring that young people feel difficult to find jobs to do, stealing crime occurrence rate increases, building poor family relationship between patients and their children. Hence the social challenge " increasing low education level young people" to any countries will cause. It is one serious social challenge to any one country government needs to attempt to implement any right or useful strategies to solve, if we hope that our future next generations can attribute their skills and efforts to serve our societies. Otherwise, our future societies will become more worse, due to our skillful and talent young people number can not increase to supply to our social different professional occupations, or shortage of professional or skillful labour number will increase to the poor countries, e.g. China, Korea, India. SO, some professional occupations, e.g. doctor, lawyer, architect, engineer , accountant, computer engineer etc. in these developing countries , they often lack enough graduates to do these occupations, because there are less number families , they can have enough money to support their next generation to continue to enroll to university to pursue to learn these any one professional subject. Also, it means that our future societies will have professional occupational jobs can not be filled enough , because many young people can not go to university to continue to learn any kinds of professional knowledge to prepare long time their career development. Hence, solving challenge of young people unemployment and training more professionals issues are needed to solve for our societies.

● Strategies solve low educational youngers feel difficulties to seek right jobs challenges

I believe that it has close relationship between our societies have many low educational young people number and unemployment rate increases. It is because the country has many low educational young people. SO, it causes unemployment rate increases because they feel difficulties to find suitable jobs to do. Hence, solving educational challenge, it will be one kind of method to solve unemployment rate increasing challenge.

Youth unemployment : The challenge and possible solutions may post complex economic, social and moral policy issues. Moreover, many families challenges may be created by increasing unemployment rate, such as economic strain, stress and mental health. Hence, any countries can not neglect that when their countries have many low educational level youngers lose jobs, they will bring unemployment rate increases, worse family relationship builds and crime rate also raises. Hence,, it is sure that it has close relationship between many youngers are low educational level and social challenges increasing number in the country.. Hence, any effective strategy must need to solve above all social challenges in order to achieve effective educational improvement to raise youngers easy seeking jobs aim. Otherwise., if
The strategy can not achieve to avoid worse family

relationship building between the unemployed low educational level youngers and their families, unemployment ratio raises, low educational level young people number increases. It is not an effective strategy to help its society to solve social and poor educational challenges.

The question is that how to solve this unemployment ratio raising or worse family relationship challenge? We need to know that their effects are caused by low educational level young people increasing number. So, solving to reduce the low educational level young people increasing number challenge, it will be the main successful factor to avoid our societies will increase more negative emotion in our future societies.

However, problem of educated and unemployment can be solved by taking following steps (i) from the very beginning, emphasis should be laid on vocational education, (ii) only those students should be allowed to seek admission in college and institutions who have some definite objectives to prosecute their studies. Youth unemployment is especially worrisome because when it is so high, it can have lasting effects on lifetime employability through the depreciation of skills and can be the cause of political instability, when the issue is common to most countries in the region, the factors behind it are not necessarily the same.

One method may be that creates business-driven solutions to economic and social challenges, it can solve the increased numbers of young people. When the society has many people like to do business, then they may create many new job positions to let the low educational level young people to work. It is one good educational development strategy to create more occupations to let low educational level young people have jobs chance.

Hence, in our future, youth unemployment is one of the biggest challenge for our global economy, how to solve it to study or activity search for a job , thus youth unemployment is running a high risk of social challenge. At the same time, social protection policies have been weakened and theme has been a fracturing of the social contact. There is a clear economic and social case for businesses to include self management, problem solving, working communication. Also, the social and labor market integration of young people is therefore a policy , what proportion of young people receive unemployment or disability benefits, it is one effective strategy to help governments to ensure businesses can create more jobs to let low educational level young people have chance to work. So, creating more low educational level jobs strategy, it can reduce low educational level young people can not find jobs to work in possible. It may be one effective social strategy to solve unemployment rate raising challenge in our future societies.

● Methods to improve educational strategy in order to let many young people have chance to learn

When on country has many low educational level young people, they will feel difficult to find right jobs to do in our societies. Then, it will bring many different kinds of social challenges. The root is due to failure educational strategy to the country. How to achieve effective educational methods to reduce the low educational level young unemployment number? I shall suggest below these educational strategies as below:

Although the challenges that education systems will face during the period. Traditionally, it has been the lower income countries that have sought, and benefits. The number if young people is rising and reaching a historial high . Increase percent of pupils reaching the expected stardard and young people ages 0 to 10 live in any poor and low income level developing countries. These strategies are supported by a number of lower challenges to draw up effective deficit recovery plans.

Closing the gap in educational achievement for children and young people living in developing countries. Their governments need to promising strategies to improve outcomes for children living in poverty . In schools , teachers pair low and high-performing pupils, and the partners work on different. At every stage of educational development, not just lowest the bar and make excuses. As young people near the end of compulsory education, it is the fluent to graduates, the total number of teachers is also needed to increase in order to satisfy future low educational level students increasing number to learn need. For example, developed country, the strategy covers the education sector in England only, although it includes to help to reduce workload, increas efficiencies, engage and encourage innovation to meet specific challenges of the poor learning effort young student, when they feel difficult to learn in classrooms. Moreover, England government would also like young people to be competent, social exclusion affect student achievement, the Ministry seeks to improve students‘ learning effort, reduces number of low achievers and raises intensive strategy for the teaching of English across. Also England schools develop a training strategy for their consideration. Benefits from adequate investment in good-quality education and skills. Everywhere, England young people with low skill levels are improved.

Hence, to the developing countries future education strategy, every child lives certain regions, but their birth number is increasing, such as Afria, China. In low and lower middle income countries, the demographic challenge is higher. So, Africa , China, low educational achievement leads to lowered economic and challenges that minority and lower social-class students face. Hence, future global skills trends, training needs and lifelong learning is needed to developing countries, labor market polarisation but constitutes a major challenge foe educations. The actionable principles listed below build on the G20 skills strategy. For examle, digitalisation is reducing demand for rountine and manual tasks when increasing demand for digitalisation industry student number. So, development to digitalisation industry will have significant needs to developing countries, e.g. ecommerce, computer industry development. Som developing country students need to learn digitalization for low income level developing countries' future education development. Also, increase the use of ICT in technology, learning and assessment to help their young people develop 21 ST century skills will have significant need to future development countries' educational strategy.

- The relationship between low educational level students increasing number and economic recession

Is the country economic recession influenced by low educational level students increasing number? If it is true, why and how low educational level students increasing number may influence the country econmic growth can not go up rapidly, even recession occurs. I shall attempt to explain the cause and effect relationship as below:

The effects of the great recession on education attainment. Why they have possible cause and effect relationship between the low educational level student increasing number and recession. In general , the decline is followed by a steep increase in graduation . In addition, although lazy educated and poor families were influenced of the recession. The number of university graduation students may be influenced by recession. Why does recession may influence low educational level students number increases or less number of university graduated student? How does recession affect student ? Another problem that students faced during the great recession was that public college, which were faced with government aid cut were forced to increase tuition. Therefore, during a period of financial crunch and unemployment, students had to pay more for graduate college or higher education.

What increase during a recession? In a recession, with rising unemployment, many may not be able to afford their mortgages, and so we can see home repossessions. This will lead to an increase in the supply of housing and less demand, for example, in the 2008 recession, US house price fell sharply because of the previous housing boom. How can recession affect schools? The adverse effects of the recession were concentrated among school districts serving higher concentrations of low-income and minority students. It means that the great recession exacerbates the inequality of student achievement outcomes.

How does economy affect education industry? A country's economy becomes more productive as the proportion of educated workers can be more efficiently carry out and tasks that require literacy and critical thinking. In this sense, education is an investment in human capital, similar to an investment in better equipment. For example, a higher education systems in serving poor populations, the number of students applying for places may be influenced to declined by 30-60% , e.g. if Africa can improve education system to be better, it ought may reduce the low educational level students number. For Africa poor populations household finance affects decisions about whether the poor families children can be educated easily, they are depended on how much Africa government's educational assistance can spend. So, if Africa government can accept to spend more expenditure on educational allowances to the poor families, then it may raise the high educational level studrnts number increases significantly.

● What are the effects of the Great Recession on education?

The decline is followed by a steep increase in graduation. There is little knowledge of the impacts on education. When some countries are experiencing recession, the number of students on free and reduced, it means that it can influence many students feel disappoint to find jobs because recession causes the number of jobs supply is decreased. So, many students won't have learning desires, then little knowledge and low educational level of students number will increase in the societies, because many young people feel education won't help them to find any jobs to do more easily when their countires are experiencing recession. Hence, recession also hurts student learning according to pioneering, higher concentrations of low income and minority students can not conclusively identify whey the recession influenced to low educational level students number increases or student indiviudal learning desire is influenced to reduce. Then, it also brings negative social influence, such as an increase in the relative number of low income workers in the recession occurring country.

As mentioned earlier, a crisis affects educational outcomes, such as how to improve educational outcomes during an economic crisis. Some economists indicated that higher education's opportunity cost falls, due to the learning desired students number reduces, during the recession occurs. Consistent with recession influencing higher education, aged 20 years or less student enrolling applications is influenced to increased only by 20% maximum. This meant that year 12 student number can be infuenced to reduce during recession. Consequently, it seems that recession has significant influence to high educated level student increasing number in any countries.

- The relationship between the increasing low educational level students number and economic growth speed

Can one country have long time increasing low educational level students number to bring its country's overall economic growth speed slowly? If it is time, whether what factors and reasons of this low educated level students long time increasing number which can influence long time slow speed economiv growth to the country, even recession effect in possible? Hence, it brings this question: Does one country have long time low educational level students increasing number, it will influence its country's overall slow economic growth or even recession effect indirectly? I shall attempt to explain as below:

Increasing low educational level students number to any one develping, e.g. Africa , China or developed, e.g. US, UK how any why it can influence the country economic growth slowly, even it can bring recession in long time. An economy's productivity rises as the number of educated workers can increase. How job training influences the country's economic development, it depends on whether the country can spend enough resource to train how many educated workers in long time. Education is often broken into specific low, primary level, middle secondary level and high university level from schools faster economic growth than countries with less educated workers.

How does education increase economic growth? A country's economy becomes more productive as the proportion of educated workers increases since educated workers can more efficiently carry out tasks that require literacy and critical thinking. In this sense, education is an investment in better equipment. How does low socioeconomic status affect education? Increasing evidence supports to link between lower learning disabilities, or other negative psychological outcomes that affect academic achievement. So, when one developing country, such as Africa, China they have low socioeconomic status, then it implies that they have many households to display learning-relative behavior problems as well as the low educated level students number will also influenced to increase , due to low socioeconomic status is causing to these both countries.

How does increasing the literacy rate impact the economy? Literacy positively impacts economic growth beyond the local community. The impact of improving literacy in students not only has a positive economic impact at a local and community level, but the productivity of the workforce low efficiency at country level too by enhancing a country's economic strength. Otherwise, when one country has economic growth, it may impact of higher education on advantage aspect, such as financing on the macro level comes out of growth, there is no crowding-effect either at the expense of less educated workers which as a result increase the number of students who can have high educated level. So, it seems that may they have close relationship between the level of cognitive skills of a nation's students has a large effect and the country's overall economic growth speed.

Sapir (2003) and Camdessus (2004) argue that the slower economic growth, it is influenced by human capital leads to an increase or decrease in the amount of skilled. So, they believe that the country's the amount of human or worker individual skill increase or decrease, it will bring indirect relationship to influence the country's economic growth speed. They believe that education and socioeconomic status have close relationship, they bring the impact of socioeconomic status on educational outcomes and reducing slow and low skills, poor economic development and learning development, low literacy to the country economic growth speed.

Hence, when the country has many low educational level youngers, it will cause slowing growth in educational development because social employers' jobs need number to the high educational level students exceeds to the high educational level students number, due to it has only low educational level students number increases , but high educational level students number decreases, which might be contributing to slower economic growth. It also implies that the effect of universities on growth is mediated through an increased supply of high educated level students number growth, there has relatively been impacted to future overall economic growth speed whether the country's economy can grow rapid or slow in long time.

On conclusion, I believe the country's economy growth speed whether is rapid or slow, it has direct or indirect relationship to be influenced by its low educational level or high educational level students increasing number factor. So, any countries can not neglect how to raise themselves countries students skills in order to let they can attribute their skills to assist themselves countries to develop in success. as well as to bring economic rapid growth effect. Otherwise, if the country can not provide excellent education system to raise high educational level students number, then it only brings long term slow economic growth effect.

CHAPTER FIVE

What is right education policy influences economic growth

Every country has different independent education policy. However, some countries' education polocy can follow another country education policy, such as Hong Kong education policy is following US some education policy, e.g. HK education system is following US educational system to implement associate degree and the establish the liberal studies subject to be an essential pass subject in high school if the student expects to enrol to any Hong Kong university to study successfully after US had implemented the accociate degree and liberal subject, it is their educational policy similar view point. But they also have different view point in this educational reform aspect, such as Hong Kong liberal studies must be one essential subject in high school. Every student must pass liberal studies subject, then they can permit to enrol HK any universities successfully. Otherwise, liberal studies subject in US high schools, students can choose this suvject to learn freely. It is one interesting selective or choice subject. This subject's pass or failure grade won't influence they can enrol to any US universities absolutely.

Anyway, HK is also following US education policy to establish or implement associate degree. It is one two to three year degree. Its education level is below than high or advance diploma , undergraduate degree in Hong Kong and US both countries. Then, it brings this question: Is HK associate degree and liberal studies subject useful to help HK students to find job or further learning more easily in HK labour market or educational system as well as the liberal studeis subject can teach as HK students to build right whole-person longlife development attitude?

I feel that the kind of HK educational reform which followed US education policy that is not one successful education reform. For recently anti -social behavior case example, HK young people choose to do violence behaviors to crash ot damage HK government legislatve building and HK police force building facilities. The liberal studies subject will encourage or persuade them to do anti-social behaviors easily, it is possible that due to HK liberal studies subject teachers educate HK students. The US freedom social policy ot strategy is right . Otherwise , HK government ought not follow China government's independent or non-freedom policy to control HK citizen's speech freedom, behavioral freedom, open-mind freedom.

So, Hk students are influenced to do anti-social behaviors as well as to do the damage behaviors to HK government police force building and HK government legisative building facilities. It seems that HK liberal studies subject teachers have responsibilities for this uissue, due to their wrong education methods influence their students to build the anti-social behavioral mind possible. Otherwise, US education policy cna help US students to develop whole-person long life development in possible, due to the liberal studeies subject if one interesting art subject. It does not concern more focus on explaining whether how to implement or what the right policy issue aspect is. It educates students how to build right analytical ability or skill to judge any matters more accurately. Otherwise, HK liberal studies subject concerns to explain whether the differences and influences between freedom countries, e.g. US, UK and non-freedom countries, e.g. China, Korea.

It can not been taught about how to raise HK student individual analytical skill or ability mainly. It focuses on teaching that HK government ought not follow China government non-freedom and independent control policy. So , it explains why some HK young people choose to do anti-social and violence behaviors in HK society suddenly.

Is HK young people anti-social behavioral performance related to how HK liberal studies subject teachers use either patience or violence teaching mind or attitude or method to teach their students? So, it has no absolute right or wrong education strategy or policy or system to any countries. It depends on whether the kind of education policy is suitable to the country social job labor market need, e.g. HK government is following US to implement associate degree in a long time. However, many HK associate degree graduated students feel difficult to find nay jobs easily as well as many HK employers preer to choose the undergraduated students , they had graduated the high/advance diploma, diploma or undergraduated degree students more than the associate degree students in HK. Because any HK employers feel these associate degree graduated students whose educational levels must be below/lower than the diploma, high/advance diploma or undergraduated degree students' educational levels. They do not give choose to let them to attempt to do their jobs more easily.

Moreover , HK's graduated students ' job supply number is shortage, but the associate degree, diploma , high/ advance diploma and undergraduate degree university students number is increasing per year. So, it explains that why the associate degree graduated students feel difficult to find any suitable jobs to do in HK society nowadays. Otherwise, US's accociate degree students won't feel more difficult to find any suitable jobs to do in US society, because its degree and non-degree level job supply number and job demand number is balance. It has any kinds of enough right skillful and ability level occupations or job natures to be provided to let any subject of associate degree graduated students to find to do in US labor market nowadays.

Hence, it explains that it has no absolute right or wrong education policy, it depends on how the country's labor market demand and supply needs in the country itself society recently, such as the case of liberal studies subject and associate degree, this educational policy is suitable in US country. But it is not suitable in HK society. It depends on the country's labor market environment, economic environment, social changing environment or social demand environment to cause whether the educational reform succeeds or fails.

Consequently, I think that liberal studies and accociate degree education reform seems to be implemented in success in US society, but it does not mean it can be implemented in sussess in HK society because it depend on different external factors. So, HK educators need to consider how to reform this educational policy issue again to satisfy students won't feel stress or psychological pressure to learn in HK, such as the case of liberal studies and associate degree, this educational policy is suitable in US society, but it is not suitable in HK society. It depends on the country's labor market environment, economic environment, social changing environment or social demand environment to cause whether the educational reform is successful or failure. Consequently, I think that liberal studies and associate degree educational policy seems to be succeeded in US society, but it does not mean it can be implemented in HK society in success because it depends on different external factors. So, HK educators need to spend time to consider how to reform this educational policy issue to satisfy HK students' real needs.

Asian and Western educating worker individual responsibility

Nowadays, Asian and Western both education policies have same or similar view points, it causes that educating worker individual responsibility to their students will have difference between Asian and Western educating workers. I shall explain as below:

Similarly, Western societies need many scientists, doctors, nurses , engineers etc. any entrepreneurs. Otherwise, Asian societies need many lawyers, accountants etc. clerical professional educating people. So, it brings the labor need market is different between Asian and Western. Also, it implies that studying any science subjects students, they can find jobs more easily in Western countries. Otherwise, studying any science subjects students, they can not find jobs more easily in Asian countries, because there are less science subjects students number demand in Asian counties. Otherwise, lawyers, accountants etc. clerical professional students will find jobs more easily in Asian countries, because Asian societies focuse on clerical professional career or job development more than science career or job development.

In Western societies, very oftn entreprensurs and scientists can do the work behind smarter machines, and develop or invent usable products , due to Western universities or large entrepreneurs, e.g. Micro-soft, Apple brands computer companies can provide enough money, time and equipment to assist scientists to attempt to invent any new usable products for future human living need. Otherwise, Western countries' education policies and business school organizations concern there will most of the benefits go e.g. researching quality land and nature resources, how intellectural property, or good ideas about what should be produced, how quality labor with unique skills. Western educators concern how to solve unskilled labor to be raised as more countries join the global economy in short time, how to educate next generation scientists to invent any intelligent-analysis machines become more powerful and more commonplace to bring the most obvious and direct beneficiaries will be the humans who are adopt at working with computer and with related devices for communications and information processing.

Western educators believe that a labor can argue the value of a major technological improvement by even a small bit, he/she will likely earn well. It means that Western educators concern how to train or educate humans with strong math and analytic skills , for example, future computers invention needs to satisfy humans who computer teachers how to teach to feel comfortable working with future computers invention , because they understand their operation and they need their computer students can be used for marketing and for other non-techic tasks.

Otherwise, Western computer teachers' education methods or attitudes do not just about teaching programming skills, it is also often about developing the hardware connected with software, understanding what kind of internet ads connect with their human viewers, or understanding what shape and color makers on iphone attractive in a given market.

Otherwise, Asian computer teachers only concern how to train computer students‘ prgramming skills, they neglect to teach computer students to create any new technological tools which can assist computer to use, such as internet high technological communication tool. So , it explains that why many computer invention is coming from Western computer scientists more than Asia computer scientists because Western computer education workers encourage computer students ought spend more time to do creative and independent analysis ability more than only learning programming writing or creative skill traditionally.

Otherwise, Asian computer education workers only concern to teach computer students to learn how to write any program. So, their creative and analysis skills or abilities will be poorer to compare Western computer students nowadays. In Western social labor market, many of their service sectors, a lot of their manufacturing, healthcare and education sector government bureaucratic employment, and their creative industries, even the military is more about manipulating advanced technology than human and job nature.

Western service industries feel one bad soldier or engineer can ruin the efforts of many others, of if someone programs the drone wrong, all sorts of problems can arise. When it comes to these complex tasks, people have to know what they are doing, they have to want to learn, and they have to want to cooperate with their fellow workers. That means that a growing technological education to service industries trend will be popular to global labor market. So, Western and Asian educators might learn how to teach studentds to learn how to teach students to learn how to apply any kinds of high technological machines knowledge to prepare to apply them in any service industries in future soon, because our societies will have many human job nature or occupations by AI (artificial intelligence) high technological tools. So, technological education will be increased to need to any countries, every country's educators need to learn many kinds of high technological knowledge in order to teach next generation to do high technological service workers in our future societies.

Our future educators need to help their students to choose right careers, because a smart young person gets a good educaton and is deciding what to do with it. Why are so many of these people going into finance, law and consulting? Smart young people from top schools can walk into high-paying jobs in these areas with relative ease, even if they do not have much or indeed any real world experience. In US labor market, they start at salaries, above the US median household income, and very quickly many of them are earning above six figures. In finance, they may be paid bonuses of million withing years at least if they come along during the right years.

There are some particular reasons why employment opportunities are growing in finance, law, and consulting. Todays, laws are more numerous and more complicated in global legal occupation market, and that increases the demand for lawyers at least at the top and of the market. Moreover, a global economy means longer supply chains , and consultants can help businesses track and evaluate these complex operations. Finance is growing in part because the promise of banks to become larger and also take on more risk.

As a general rule, the age structure of achievement is being upward, due to specialization and the growth of knowledge. Mathematicians used to prove theorems at age twenty, but now it happens at age thirty, because there are many students feel interesting to learn space science, biology, chemical, engineering, architectural , building science. All of these subjects will need the students to learn how to apply math to solve any learning problems.

So, Asian and Western educators need to concern that law, finance, math subjects will be popular learning subjects to our students, instead of science subject. Our educators have responsibilities to learn much extra knowledges concern these subjects in order to raise these subject students' learning level and learning quality successfully, because future any one kind of occupations demand will be predicted to increase. So, it implies that any one subject of these teachers' teaching performance will be also needed to raise. If our eduators expect excellent professionals to be trained to any one of above these occupations successfully in our societies.

● The differences between Asia and Western successful education system

What is the successful education policy or system? It has no absolute right answer. Because every country has different job need, learning environment, learning attitude needs to itself country students. So, it is difficult to evaluate whether how to implement one education system or policy. It can be applied to any countries' learning environment successfully. However, I shall indicate every country will have these similar learning environments need view points in order to let educators know whether how ought need to implement any education policys more easily. The factors may include as below:

(1) In order to capitalize on the increasing demand for higher level education and continuous upskilling, universities, traditionally slow to adapt will need to reinvent themselves. When those universities less willing to adapt will suffer, those prepared to innovate will succeed. They will need to ensure a stronger connection between what is being taught and what the market is looking for, when maintaining the which will become more important commercially to universities as well as they may need to change the range or courses on offer, their length and how they are taught to allow for easier learning. This new approach will require learning-enhancing buildings which encourage and facilities collaboration and socializing.

(2) Universities need to build new facilities which will need to understand the needs of the next generation of students and the requirements of smart, digital campuses and accommodation equipped with intelligent facilities. They will have to effectively interpret the date , they collect and use it to enhance the student learning experience, creating an effective learning experience creating an effective digital learning environment and personalized

individual learning experiences.

(3) Universities, especially these with significant focus on research, not only a part on helping improve the country poor productivity, but also have a critical role in development economic growth that goes beyond unskilling the next generation and directly employing, recent graduated students. They also generate growth in the communities around them: creating social value and making an impact locally. They drive the innovation that leads to growth, developing new technologies and products, collaborating with businesses in generate new ideas, facilitating knowledge transfer all increasing leadning to business start-ups and supporting businesses as they grow. The sector is a source of skills, innovation and exports in its own right. The important role places universities at the heart of the economy.

(4) Internationalisation of education system / policy. Internationalisation will be one core component of future high education, such as many global universities rely on income from international ventures as well as the diversity that overseas students bring to their compuses, most wish to attract and retain overseas talent, many collaborate with institutions elsewhere in the world, some engage internationally as part of wider institutional commitment to social responsibility and others have , or seek to establish branch compuses overseas.

In conclusion, any country needs to follow itself students‘ learning need, economic environment and labor supply and demand environment need to design the most effective educational policy to satisfy its primary , secondary and university students' learning needs more absolute.

What are the differences between Asia and Western liberal studies teaching aims and influences

What is the meaning of " liberal studies" ? Liberal studies subject is related to " liberal act", " liberal education" or " general education", in asia or foreign education system. Liberal means acts or sciences, pursuits, occupations whether which is suitable to persons of superior social status, general intellectual enlargement, it is required of technical or professional training.

Paris and Kimball (2000, 144) defines liberal education means that becoming multicultural, eveluating general education and integration, rather than specialization, promoting the commonweal and citizenship, regarding all levels of education or belonging to a common enterprise, reconceiving teaching as stimulating learning and inquiring, promoting the formation of values and the practice of service and employing assessments.

However, some educators argue to bring different vieww points, they feel liberal studies subject does not only mean arts or sciences. They remark that students in the USa lack the broad foundation of knowledge necessary to cope with post industrial society and maintains that there is a need to develop " courses in the humanities, social science and natural sciences that challenge young people to think synthetically and to understand that the essence of education is the courage and ability to make value judgements.

Hence foreign high schools hope liberal studies can train every student to make personal judgement and analysis ability to decide to make any matters more accurate. Also, it explains why foreign high schools permit high school students to select this liberal studies subject to study.

Because foreign high schools feel taht this subject is one free choice interesting subject. Some students won't feel that teaching hoe to make personal judgement and analysis , which will not bring useful knowledge to help them to find any jobs to do or they feel that social any occupations won't need to learn liberal studies knowledge or this subject does not relate to help their career development.

Otherwise, in some asian countries , such as Hong Kong , high schools feel that this subject is not only interesting subject, it is art subject. These Hong Kong schools feel this liberal studies can develop in learners open mindedness, rational thinking, citizenship, multiculturalism and the ability to make value judgements and it should also promote the integration of useful knowledge and involve the use of enquiry for teaching. So, it explains that why Hong Kong high schools must need have this liberal studies subject to be taught and students must be learnt to pass in order to enrol any universities to study successfully.

Hong kong high schools feel this subject must help students to be trained to make more accurate judgement and accurate analysis mind and skills. If the Hong Kong high schools have mone this subject to be taught to learn its students to learn. Then, the high school students can not confirm or ensure they own accurate judgement and analysis skills or abilities to prepare their further occupation development or carrer development successfully. For example, recently Hong Kong many high school students who are persuaded to force to crash Hong Kong government legislative building and Hong Kong police force building as well as they bring crowd to stay on driving roads to cause traffic jam, even any buses, taxies, cars, lorries , trams etc. transportation tools can not be driven to go through any driving roads absolutely.

Hence, this liberal studies subject can bring negative influence to Hong Kong liberal studies learning students to encourage them to do the anti-social behaviors when themselves feel dissatisfactory or sad or unhappy to Hong Kong government's policy implementation nowadays. It reflects or implies that Hong Kong liberal studies subject teachers had persuaded or they had encouraged these Hong Kong high school students to to anti-social behaviors easily. If Hong Kong high schools chose liberal studies subject was on select (choice) subject or withdraw this subject must be taught in schools. Then, I believe that Hong Kong students won't choose to do anti-social behaviors to complaint their Hong Kong government more easier, because Hong Kong liberal studies high school teachers ' anti-socail psychology will influence how their teaching attitudes to be taught to their students as well as how they teach anti-society or anti-Hong Kong government knowledge to let their students to learn or their teaching behaviors will influence their students ought do anti-social behaviors, it is right after this liberal studies course is finished. Consequently, their Hong Kong students will raise anti-social feeling and they will be persuaded or encouraged to do anti-social behaviors to complaint their Hong Kong government , such as recently many Hong Kong young people had planned to attack or damage Hong Kong legislative building and Hong Kong police force headquarter building. Also, their anti-social behaviors are implemented consequently and it causes Hong Kong polices need to threaten these Hong Kong young peoples' anti-social behaviors. So, liberal studies subject may influence Hong Kong students to choose to do anti-social behaviors more easily. I think that Liberal education does that by teaching students to become lifelong learners who are their own best teachers. It enables them to take intellectual risks and to think laterally -- to understand how the humanities, the arts and the sciences inform, enrich and affect one another. By connecting diverse ideas and themes across the academic disciplines, liberal arts students learn to better reason and analyze, and express their creativity and their ideas.

Why does liberal studies become a core subject to Hong Kong high schools? In addition to liberal studies , there are three other core subjects in Hong Kong educational system, such as Chinese language, English language and mathematics in Hong Kong education system. Traditionally, languages have been considered as tools not only for communication, but also for learning, such as english language must be learnt to Hong Kong students, because they need to write english to do their homeworks, assignments, they need to listen english when their teachers choose to use english language to teach their students in classrooms as well as they also need to read any english books. So, english subject must be one essential subject to be taught to any Hong Kong primary, secondary, and university students nowadays.

But, why will liberal subject be a core subject in Hong Kong schools? Before 2009, liberal studies subject was never a core subject at any level in Hong Kong, but when Hong Kond education reforms which started at the end of the 20 th century. One of the key elements is curriculum reform, in relation to which the curriculum development council published learning to learn life learning and whole-person development (curriculum development council , 2001).

Hong Kong education system began to promote a willingness to learn throughout one's life and the capacity to engage in such learning in one of the key aims of the curriculum reform. In most cases, Hong Kong educators felt lifelong leaning involves learning by oneself, outside schools and institutes and in this sense it is closely related to independent learning. They also felt that liberal studies subject compares other subjects, it may be unique in its potential contribution to train Hong Kong students to raise in order to achieve aim to own more independent learning capability and lifelong learning as Hong Kong students and expected to engage in a variety of enquires and carry out an independent project.

So, Hong Kong eduators believed liberal studies subject can bring the good idea of whole-person development, promotion of moral and civic education and it is a response to the useful of learning knowledge to train Hong Kong young people to achieve one perfect whole-person development before they enter Hong Kong society to work further. So , it explains that why Hong Kong high students must need liberal studies subject to be a core subject to be taught to let students to learn as well as they must pass this subject if they expected to enrol to any Hong Kong universities to study successfully further. Otherise, foreign high schools feel this liberal studies subject is only one select (choice) subject, because they feel thay some students won't have much interest to learn this subject, it is only common act subject and it is not same to psychological subject in universities or it is one occupational choice (select) subject in relation to raise whole-person development to every student absolutely. So, it explains why it brings the difference between select (choice 0 and essential subject of liberal studies learning to asian and foreign high school students nowadays.

In Hong Kong liberal studies subject learning aim aspect, Hong Kong educators believe that liberal studies subject can bring these advantages to young people. They believe that liberal studies subject will foster students‘ capacity for life-long learning, so that it can train them to face the challenges of the future with confidence. Moreover, lifelong learning is not limited to a set of independent learning skills, but is a culture, such as Chinese culture of how one should position oneself in our changing world. So, Hong Kong liberal studies subject main teaching aim may include: Training every student's personal lifelong learning attitude, building Chinese lifelong learning culture, awareness of continue learning is essential, active relevant ,and continupus, training them to apply high technological learning tools, training their learning attitudes are influenced on focus is on the how more than the what, training they demonstrate information literacy, inquiries are nurtured and training them to take responsibility for their learning. So, Hong Kong educators expect to train or build Hong Kong students have good learning attitudes and building Chinese lifelong learning culture to Hong Kong next generation.

However, Hong Kong liberal studies subject aims to help students to understand issues faced by society and to respect different opinions. Liberal studies teachers expect to train their these skills to be improved, such as generic skills, these are a high demand for generic skills in Hong Kong society, in which the economy is knowledge based liberal studies brings great emphasis on the development of such skills for meeting Hong Kong societal needs. The idea that generic skill affect performance in a wide range of functioning is by no means a new concept. Liberal studies is expected to be taught how good cooperating to do any tasks or projects or assignments, when students need to cooperate with colleagues in complex environment of work. Generic skills can not operate without knowledge, such as building s bridge needs have engineering knowledge or writting an essay needs have vocabilary and grammer of the language knowledge. Hence, generic skills are supported to be transferable skills which effort performance in many.

Also, liberal studies subject can teach communication skills, when a classroom learning and teaching activity is needed to group discussion in classroom as well as when students are insolved in enquiry or an issue , they will usually work in small groups and so group discussion becomes essential . So, liberal studies subject can be taught to train students how to understand of turn-raking, the ability to identify others' viewpoints and an appreciation that every one's views should be respected most easily. It can train collaborative skills, how to help students to engage effectively in tasks and teamwork. Because group work can be used to develop not only students' communication skills, but also their ability to cooperate effectively with others. When Hong Kong students can learn liberal studies subject, then when they explore on issue in groups , they can have more confidence to work with classmates in making decisions on, for example, how to analyze the sorts of information needed to finish any tasks more easily and how it can be collected and organized more easily. Also, liberal studies subject can train students how to negotiate and argue move towards a consensus more easily. Liberal studies subject can train students to raise critical thinking skills, such as how to help them to draw out meaning from given data or statements, generate and evaluate arguments, and train them to make more accurate judgement to finish any matters or tasks more easily and effectively and efficiently. This is the teaching aims of liberal studies subject in Hong Kong high schools nowadays.

However, Hong Kong educators also believe liberal studies subject can train these skills to high school students, such as problem solving skills, how to understand the problem to note the existing data and constraints and see what is needed to solve it more easily, how to formulate a plan, carry out the plan and check it by confirmation of each relevant test at each stage and to check the solution to see if it can be improved more easily, creatie skills, liberal studies can engage students in investigation in groups to develop and evaluate solutions to various problems through such activities, it is possible that liberal studies can train students learn how to create a creative environment to provide them to raise the more ability to generate original ideas and solve problems more easily, liberal studies lessons can train students hoe to see, analyse, manage easily and present information critically in an intelligently information age and a digitised world.

However, the aim difference of the liberal studies subject between Asian and Western is that Western liberal studies subject is only concentrate on art interesting aspect, e.g. focusing on social and personal psychological research, music , historical , social science knowledge researchs. Otherwise, Asian liberal studies subject focuses on whole-person development aspect, e.g. training students how to improve itself country residents' quality of life, learning how the country's residents participate in political and social affairs with rights and responsibilities with respect to the rule of law, learning how to demonstrate a sound understanding of the key idea, concepts and terminologies of the subject as well as developing the capacity to construct knowledge through enquiring into contemporary issues with affect themselves, their society, their nation, the human world and physical environment, learning how to reflect on the development of Asian youngers' own multiple identifies, value systems and world views with respect to personal experiences, social and cultural contexts and the impacts of developments in science, technology and globalization, learning how to identify the values of different views and judgements on personal and social issues and how to apply critical thinking skills, creativity and different perspectives in making decisions and judgements on issues and problems at both how to present arguments clearly and demonstrate respect for evidence, and open-mindedness and tolerance towards the views and values held by other people, learning how to develop skills related to enquiry learning , including self-management skills, problem-solving skills, communication skills, information processing skills, and skills in using information and communication technology, learning how to carry out self-directed learning which includes the processes of selling goals, making and implementating drawing conclusions, reporting findings and conducting evaluation skills, learning how to demonstrate an appreciation for the values of their own and other cultures, and for values, and be committed to becoming responsible and conscientious citizen in themselves countries.

Given the global leadership of American higher education, and the global economy's demands for flexible, adaptable employees, undergraduate liberal education is more than relevant. It remains one of our country's great assets. Is it for everyone? Of course not. But for those who pursue liberal arts education, it can be life transforming.Thus, it explains although western countries and asia countries both have liberal studies subject to be taought in high schools and universities , but liberal studies subject is only select (choice) subject to western countries' high schools because this subject is not focus in whole-persone development, it is only interesting subject, such as any act subjects in western countries' educational system. Otherwise, asia countries consider liberal studies subject is one essential subject in high schools because asia countries feel it can train every youngers' whole person development skills to prepare their further possible unpredictive any challenge facing solving ability when they work in society. So, the difference views of this subject is that liberal studies subject is only one short time interesting learning subject to let students to choose to study in western high schools, but otherwise, this subject is one long time whole -person development learning knowledge to prepare their further social work development life period or career period. Hence, it explains that short time learning interest view and long time whole-person development view both to which can influence that whether liberal studies subject is one essential subject or one select (choice) subject between asia and western high schools nowdays.

The differences between Asia and Western Liberal studies advantages and disadvantages

What Is Liberal Studies? Liberal studies, also known as liberal arts, comprises a broad exploration of social sciences, natural sciences, humanities, and the arts. If you are interested in a wide-ranging education in humanities, communication, and thinking, read on to find out about the educational and career possibilities in liberal studies. Schools offering Liberal Arts degrees can also be found in these popular choices. People often assume "liberal arts" is a political term. As it's used in academia it's closer to the idea of broadening the mind and "liberating" it from parochial divisions and unthinking prejudice. It encourages the questioning of assumptions and reliance on facts as well as an understanding that even facts can be interpreted differently through different lenses. Ideally, it enables individuals to gather information, interpret it, and make informed decisions on a wide variety of topics.It's not just the "soft" subjects like English and sociology that constitute a liberal arts education. People often talk about STEM (Science, Technology, Engineering and Math) courses, as totally separate from "liberal arts" courses. They think of "science" as "real" in a way that anthropology or art history are not: an atom is an atom, after all. But scientific phenomena are also subject to interpretation and debate as they are observed and theories are created and tested. Even a cursory knowledge of evolutionary theory or the light as wave/particle debate demonstrates that point.

The "hard" sciences are ways of seeing the world and trying to understand how it works just as much as psychology or political science are. A good liberal arts curriculum puts students in touch not just with ways of interpreting the world around us but also with the fact that the world can be "interpreted" in the first place. Ultimately, it tries to help us understand our place in it and our relationships with each other.

Degree Levels Bachelor's, master's and Ph.D. Concentrations American Studies, Humanities, International Affairs, Social and Public Policy Common Courses Writing, Social Foundations, Environmental Studies, Global Cultures Online Availability Full- and part-time online programs available. You may be required to complete some courses on-campus. Median Salary (2018) $78,470 (Postsecondary Teachers), Job Outlook (2016-2026) 15% (Postsecondary Teachers)U.S. Bureau of

Labor Statistics (BLS) .

What is a Liberal Studies Program?

Liberal studies programs culminate in associate's or bachelor's degrees. Classes in anthropology, art, music, ethnic studies, psychology, sociology, literature, philosophy, communications and most other departments in the humanities will count towards a liberal studies degree. Some possible career options with this degree include elementary school teacher, retail store manager, minister or a public relations specialist. The table below outlines some general requirements for these career options. Undergraduate degree programs in liberal studies and liberal arts involve core and elective coursework in a variety of subjects, including history, cultural studies, art, philosophy, religion, literature, and the natural sciences. In general, the goal of a liberal studies program is a strong, basic foundation of knowledge and skills that will support an array of careers and interests. Some programs allow you to develop your own path of coursework based on your interests, while others offer concentrations in areas such as early education or performing arts.

It is one interesting question: Does liberal studies only bring advantages, but it has none any disadvantages. It seems to research how to live in Mars planet destination question. Although, human provides suitable living envioronment to let us to live, instead of our earth. Research Mars planet to live, it is one worth research , but we can not guarantee whether Mras planet will bring what disadvantages to let us to live in possible, when ww really live in Mars planet in future one day, the disadvantages may include, for example, whether Mars planet's weather environment is suitable to human to live in long time, during ir is very cool at night or very hoe in some places, the trouble is the pole areas get as cold as -195 degree and are prone to storms that make landing even harder. It is also not a very exciting place, the northern plains of Mars are pretty that and boring. The equational region mostly stays above -100 degree and can reach 20 degree. It also has more sunlight that astronauts could harvest for solar power, rearely gets storms and has all sorts of interesting terrain to explore. But it does not seem to have much, if any accessible water, or whether Mars planet's lands can be built in stable. Any houses won't be damages from unpredictable bad geographical environment influence easily. Mars planet travellers are about to face the most dangerous part of their journey, the trouble with landing on Mars is that its atmosphere is almost non-existent, it is 160 times less dense than Earth's , on average . This means , but because gravity on Mars is stronger than that on the moon, we would need a lot more boosters. This means we will probably need a combination of boosters and something to create drag.

Hence, once Mars researchers are down, the explorers will be struking around for a whike . Even if they are not establishing a permanent settlement. They will have to wait months at a minimum for Earth and Mars to come into a alignment again, so they can travel home in a matter of months rather than years. There is no visiting Mars without setting up a base.

Why I concern that liberal studies subject whether it can bring advantages only, it seems to Mars planet living research whether Mars can bring more advantages to let us to live to replace Earth. This question seems to ask whether liberal studies can assist students to raise any skills or abilities to be trained to learn other subjects more easily, or training their judgement, analysis abilities to be raised

or training to be whole person development absolutely in order to achieve these all positive advantages absolutely or this subject can not bring positive advantages to assist students to learn any other subjects more easily absolutely. In general, in a liberal studies curriculum brigs these benefits, students sharpen their reading and writing skills by completing research papers. You also practice verbalizing your ideas through classroom discussions and learn to develop multiple perspectives. Other skills developed include: Critical and analytical thinking, effective communication, reasoning and problem solving. What careers that students can attempt to seek after they had graduated liberal studies degree in university? A liberal studies education doesn't prepare you for only one specific career; instead, the skills you learn in a liberal studies program can be beneficial in multiple professions. Solid writing and communication skills are paramount to most positions, and the critical-thinking skills you learn can be applied to any field that requires analytical thought, such as business or education. Other possible career areas include the following: Sales and marketing,
nonprofit organization director, journalist,
education administration, politician, college recruiter, urban planner/city manager etc. positions. Also, liberal studies graduated students could choose a writing-intensive career as a columnist, editor or research assistant. Businesses often hire liberal studies graduates as customer service and relations personnel, coordinators and consultants, who then may advance towards management and executive positions. Many lobbyists, politicians, creative writers, speech writers, journalists and archivists have all started careers with a liberal studies education. A liberal studies degree can also be applied towards a master's

degree, and a future career in education or a variety of other fields.

Liberal studies programs offer a way for you to strengthen almost any career skills you want. The independent nature of your degree, along with courses in communications, can help you develop your work ethic and teamwork skills. Literature and foreign language classes may enhance your abilities to read and write critically, self-motivate and speak publicly. Classes in the social sciences can sharpen your analytical skills, familiarizing you with data cohorts and statistical models. At a real-world internship, you'll be given a chance to advance and test these skills while you learn to network.

According to the U.S. Bureau of Labor Statistics (BLS) there are a wide variety of careers available to those who pursue a liberal studies degree and therefore, an equally wide salary range. For example, a retail store manager makes a median annual income of $38,310 in 2015, but a public relations specialist or an elementary school teacher make considerably more - $56,770 and $54,550, respectively. However, teachers require licensure in their state of residence and therefore, additional education. The same is true of those who pursue a career in the ministry or clergy - while some denominations only require a bachelor's degree and some on-the-job training, other denominations prefer a master's degree in ministry leadership. Liberal Studies is meant to allow students to develop an open mind through critical thinking. Students are introduced to a host of issues and are then taught to look at the issue from different perspectives. But many teachers force their students to follow a particular writing style or stick to model answers. And most students do so, because they are scared they will be penalised in terms of marks if they don't. This defeats the whole purpose of Liberal Studies. If we are learning to express our opinions, why should we follow model answers?

Such as Hong Kong liberal studies advantages and disadvantages case study, Hong Kong lineral studies is core subject. It aims to link up knowledge of all subjects. HK education proposal is 3 years in junior school, 3 years in senior high school and 4 years in university. It aims to link up knowledge, such as economic, geography. Is it benefit to HK students? What are the advantages and disadvantages of the subject itself brought to HK students? Is it advisable to include liberal studies as a core subject in HK education system in 2008 year on teaching material and teacher's supply preparation aspect?

Liberal Studies is meant to train our critical thinking skills. But when we look at the exam, we don't see how that's implemented. We are asked questions that seem to require fixed answers, according the marking scheme. I always thought the marking scheme was there just for reference, but we are confined to giving the exact ideas provided in the scheme.I think there needs to be better communication between the Hong Kong Examinations and Assessment Authority, the Education Bureau, the markers and the teachers about what exactly they want from the students. Do they want facts, or do they want our opinions? They keep saying the subject aims to improve our critical thinking, but I don't feel the current system helps us improve in that area.

I think we need to link the goal to the method by which it is achieved. I believe the failure in doing this is one of the main reasons British and American universities ignore

Liberal Studies grades when making offers to students.What the HKEAA led us to believe about Liberal Studies wasn't really the full picture. For a start, there are hidden model answer formats that mean if students misinterpret some words in the question, a heavy penalty is imposed.What's more, students have to think and write unbelievably fast to complete the paper, as there are so many questions. How can students master the skills needed to answer Liberal Studies questions? Our current method of "learning by doing" does not apply to this subject.

Hong Kong some liberal studies students , they feel learning challenges to study this subject. They indicated that the biggest problem with Liberal Studies is that it is an exam-based subject. As such, lots of teachers and students focus more on acquiring the skills necessary to answer the questions than on discussing current affairs. Instead of developing students' interest in current affairs, this only strengthens exam skills. It would be better if Liberal Studies was more coursework-based than exam-based. Otherwise, other some different view point liberal studies students indiated that they feel these challenges concern liberal studies learning thatI don't think it's fair that it is a core subject that is forced upon students. While it is important to have some knowledge of current affairs, we shouldn't be examined on our understanding of social issues. Some students at my school didn't get in to university because they didn't pass this subject at DSE level.

Of course, no reference to free speech is complete without also acknowledging the mechanism by which it is exercised. Social media and technology have been a decidedly mixed blessing in promoting civil discourse. Read the comments section on just about any news story having to do with one of America's top liberal arts schools, and you'll find no shortage of trolls and vitriolic anti-intellectualism.The value of a liberal arts education. they received an outstanding liberal arts education as an undergraduate, and it continues to shape their career and life. They firmly believe liberal education is the best preparation a young person can have for the job market and a rewarding, meaningful life as a citizen of our democracy.

However, HK educators identified some advantages and disadvantages of liberal studies to HK students. The advantages may include; Helping students to build ip own points of view, cultivating students' critical thinking skill, preventing students‘ single track approach, due to the specialization in secondary subjects, broadening students' knowledge base, increasing students‘ learning incentive, providing an integration of knowledge of all subjects mutually, providing the future generation with wider knowledge use, independent thinking, creativity in a knowledge oriented society and enabling students to obtain a life long benefits.

But, it also brings disadvantages, they may include: No definite textbook of liberal studies, leading to strong contrast and confrontation between liberal studies and traditional subjects, it may become a new burden or learning pressure to the student, unfairness may result as there is no standard answer in assessment of liberal studies. Also, many HK educators feel that it is not possible to include liberal studie as core subject, the reasons may include: It lacks cautious plan, housing building on Mars land technological skill, food growing technolgical skill, preventing unpredictive bad weather change on Mars technological skill before the Mars living planning will decide to implement. So, Hong Kong liberal studies disadvantages include , it lacks a comprehensive training of teachers, can not be alloweded to be trained within a limited period of 35 hours. Hence, HK liberal studies teaching implement needs have enough time to research to work out what training best fits teachers, what teaching resources must need to provide. It seems to the Mars living research implementation plan. Before ,any countries need to implement any liberal studies subject , they need to find what weaknesses or challanges they are facing to achieve this liberal studies subject as well as they also need to find any solutions to solve the challanges to threaten the liberal studies subject to be implemented. If they neglect how to solve any challenges they will face to implement liberal studies subject, then they will encounter failure to implement the liberal studies subject to let young people to learn in their schools unsuccessfully.

In conclusion, a liberal arts education can be very frustrating. It forces students to see multiple viewpoints and continually challenge their own. It removes the comfort of assuming there are "right" answers to big questions, that civilization moves in a linear fashion or that facts are facts no matter who looks at them. But it also introduces students to the pleasures of debate and the ever-expanding world of ideas. It opens doors, enabling the mind to go wherever it wants in the pursuit of knowledge and understanding. It bends toward openness instead of containment.In times of great division, the capacity to see others' viewpoints and the imperative to assess one's own become more and more important. A liberal arts education works for us, no matter what our political leanings are. We need it now more than ever.College students who major in the humanities always get asked a certain question. They're asked it so often—and by so many people—that it should come printed on their diplomas. That question, posed by friends, career counselors, and family, is “What are you planning to do with your degree?” But it might as well be “What are the humanities good for?”It is possible that liberal studies can help students to solve whys and hows of human behavior in their daily life more easily.What matters now is not the skills you have but how you think. Can you ask the right questions? Do you know what problem you’re trying to solve in the first place? Educator argues for a true “liberal arts” education—one that includes both hard sciences and “softer” subjects. A well-rounded learning experience, he says, opens people up to new opportunities and helps them develop products that respond to real human needs. Summarily, liberal studies can bring students these benefits after their learning experience, such as: 1. To build the concept of "valuable learning" from the various meanings that college students gave to it when they were asked about their opinion of the valuable things they learned in liberal education courses they have taken as part of their curriculum. 2. To approach to the ways students think and feel about liberal education, so those educational approaches with greater learning potential could be strengthened. The instrument used to collect students? 3. Training students how to collect, classify, analyze and interpret multiple answers that students gave any questions allowed a better understanding of the impact of the liberal education courses.

Liberal studies subject need
differences between Asia and Western
What is a Liberal Arts Education? Working towards a baccalaureate degree in the Arts or Sciences involves taking courses in what are traditionally referred to as the "liberal"

arts. This means that your courses will be in general areas of study--philosophy, mathematics, literature, art history, economics, languages, and so on--rather than in applied or specialized fields. A liberal arts education is not intended to train you for a specific job, though it does prepare you for the world of work by providing you with an invaluable set of employability skills, including the ability to think for yourself, the skills to communicate effectively, and the capacity for lifelong learning.

What Will I Study as Part of an Arts Education? You will study a variety of subjects, looking at the world and its people from various points of view. You will learn about ideas and beliefs that have guided human beings and shaped civilizations for thousands of years. What does it mean to be human? What have humans done, thought about, and felt? What is truth and beauty, and what are their value to life? How have we been shaped by, and how have we shaped, our physical and natural environment? What skills, methods or techniques can be used to examine the world and its people? These are some of the key questions examined by the Arts disciplines.

A liberal arts education is by nature broad and diverse, rather than narrow and specialized. Choosing courses from many disciplines gives you a wide and useful education. In the first year, an Arts student normally takes a variety of introductory courses. This not only gives you a wide knowledge of subjects but helps you to choose certain areas for further study. In most cases, you will be encouraged to take courses in at least some of the major categories within the liberal arts: Humanities (English Literature, Modern Languages, History, Philosophy), Social Sciences (Anthropology, Economics, Geography, Political Science, Sociology), Creative Arts (Fine Art, Theatre, Speech,

Creative Writing), and the Sciences. At the same time, Arts programs usually allow for some degree of specialization in a Major discipline or in a group of thematically-linked courses. By concentrating on a given subject, whatever it may be, you will go beyond the mere surface of things and gain a solid grasp of the core material in a given area.

Why Should I Pursue an Arts Education?
This is the big question: Why Arts? Why not Engineering? Or Nursing? Or Heavy Duty Mechanics? Or Computing Science? There are numerous ways to answer this question, and ultimately the utility of any answer will depend upon your own circumstances. For you, studies in the Arts may provide the necessary practical skills that you will apply on the job; or they may prepare you to move on to a graduate or professional school. For others, the key value of a liberal arts education may be the personal satisfaction and fulfillment that studying philosophy or art makes possible. Still others will be able to excel in today's global business world because the foreign language skills developed in their Arts education gave them an important edge. Indeed, the reasons for pursuing a liberal arts education are as many as the number of potential students. What you need to ask is what you want to get out of a postsecondary education. If you want to get a solid, broadly-based, general education which will improve your analytical, communication and learning abilities, then the liberal arts may be for you.

What About Skills Training?You have probably heard a lot of talk lately about how important it is to get the proper "skills set" so that you can be immediately attractive to an employer. Some think that the goal of a postsecondary education should be to provide you with as much specific training as possible before you arrive on the job, thus relieving potential employers of the costs and risks associated with hiring untrained workers. In light of this perception, many students balk at taking general liberal arts courses and choose instead to focus narrowly on a vocational or professional area of study. This can be an excellent choice. There are many rewarding and fulfilling careers that one can pursue with the help of a first-class vocational or career training program. But make sure that you are making your educational choices for the right reasons—those that are best for you. If you are shying away from Arts courses because you think that you need training in specific skills to get a job, you may be mistaken. First, a liberal arts education does provide you with tangible, practical skills that employers value highly. What is more, you will obtain skills and knowledge that are never obsolete. The world is changing rapidly and there may be a danger in preparing yourself too narrowly to fit a certain slot that may not even exist by the time you get into the job market. Meanwhile, the underlying skills, abilities and attributes fostered in the Arts are always relevant.

Why does liberal studies subject need to learn in some countries? What factors will raise its teaching and learning need to any countries ? I shall explain the possible factors to influence its learning and teaching as below:

Any students and teachers want to know why you need to learn liberal studies. I don't admire or count as worthwhile any study which aims at making money for this subject. Such studies are just hiring out our talents and are only of value if they train the mind and do not pre-occupy it. We should only spend time on them as long as the mind has nothing better to do, as they our apprenticeship, not our proper work. You can see why liberal studies are so called: they are worthy of a free man. But only one study is truly liberal in making a man free, and that is the study of wisdom, with is strength of purpose and its noble and exalted ideals.

Liberal education does not have an easily identifiable essence. . . . But the fact is that no other form of education is capable of so thoroughly examining universal or even particularistic existential and moral issues. No other form of education is able to concentrate on the most important questions of how life is to be lived or how it is to be lived in relation to other lives. Liberal education offers the intellectual and emotional basis on which is constructed a capacity to make decisions. It is the means by which men and women have sought to interpret the world or to take a comprehensive view of it. . . . The inevitable conclusion is that the telltale identifying marks of a liberal education are the manner in which a subject is taught or learned, the spirit in which it is offered, and the attitudes that may just result from the teaching and learning.

Nowadays, we live in a culture divided between two conceptions of a liberal education. The older one is the idea of an education that is liberalis, "fitted for freedom," in the sense that it is aimed at freeborn gentlemen of the propertied classes. This education initiated the elite into the time-honored traditions of their own society; it sought continuity and fidelity, and discouraged critical reflection. The "new" idea interprets the word liberalis differently. An education is truly "fitted for freedom" only if it is such as to produce free citizens, citizens who are free not because of wealth or birth, but because they can call their minds their own. Male and female, slave-born and freeborn, rich and poor, they have looked into themselves and developed the ability to separate mere habit and convention from what they can defend by argument. They have ownership of their own thought and speech, and this imparts to them a dignity that is far beyond the outer dignity of class and rank.

Nussbaum, Martha Craven (1997) explains that this liberal studies subject will not be uncritical moral relativists – for ownership of one's own mind usually yields the understanding that some things are good and some bad, some defensible and other indefensible, for they know that in tradition lies much that has stood the test of time, that should command people's respect. They will start from convention and tradition when they ask what they should choose, viewing it as essential food for the mind. On the other hand, they do not confuse food with the strength in the mind that the food is supposed to produce. They know they need to use tradition to invigorate their own thought – but this benefit involves a willingness to criticize it when criticism is due. They do not prize custom just because of its longevity, nor do they equate what has been around a long time with what must be or with what is "natural." In general, the liberal studies students therefore want to learn a great deal about other ways and people – both in order to establish respectful communication about matters of importance and in order to continue rethinking their own view about what is best. In this way, they hope to advance from the cultural narrowness into which we all are born toward true world citizenship.

Why does need to learn education in the Liberal Arts ?

A liberal arts education has at its center four practices that distinguish it from other kinds of learning: critical thinking, examination of life, encounters with difference, and free exchange of ideas. By offering an education in the liberal arts, some liberal studies subject teachers believe that the importance of lifelong learning characterized by sustained intellectual curiosity and an open mind for assessing the unfamiliar. At the same time, by using critical thinking to identify assumptions, to test logic, to evaluate evidence, to reason correctly, and to take responsibility for the conclusions and actions that result, a student of the liberal arts can grow personally as well as intellectually. A liberally educated person should be capable of principled judgment, seeking to understand the origins, context, and implications of any area of study, rather than looking exclusively at its application. A liberally educated person should also be skilled at solving problems, drawing together multiple perspectives in the creation of new knowledge.

Because knowledge is lost if it is not shared, both students and teachers of the liberal arts strive to engage in precise and graceful communication. This communication takes place verbally, but also in other ways, including the symbolic and expressive systems of mathematics, music, computer languages, the natural sciences, and the visual and performing arts. By learning and exploring these systems, one may attain an understanding of aspects of human expression, which is a crucial part of liberal education. Otherwise, some liberal studies subject teachers argue that the central task of liberal education is to activate each student's mind, so that choices and actions may emerge from independent thought rather than from acceptance of conventional assumptions or dictates.

Hence, liberal studies subject brings some educational system changing to some countries, such as Hong Kong educational system, it becomes one essential one essential subject in high school, any high school students must pass this subject if they expect to enrol to any Hong Kong universities successfully. It will bring negative psychological pressure to Hong Kong students in fact. This flexibility places significant responsibility on each student to design a coherent and compelling course of study, in conversation with a faculty adviser. Each student declares an academic major at some point during the first four semesters of enrollment. In consultation with an adviser, the student plans a comprehensive program that can incorporate options such as mentored research, off-campus study, teaching certification, an internship, or an interdisciplinary concentration. The academic major gives a distinctive shape to the four years of undergraduate education. At the same time, it is important for Hong Kong students to balance exploration and focus in their nonmajor choices. Hong Kong students need to design a program of study outside the major that reflects thoughtful planning and is consistent with their goals. Working closely with the academic adviser, the Hong Kong students need to develop a provisional four-year plan that reflects the diversity of academic disciplines while incorporating study at the advanced level in one or more fields. The provisional plan usually requires revision, but with each change the student and adviser consider how the plan reflects the student's evolving sense of what it means to be liberally educated. Morwover, Hong Kong student and advisers will need to discuss areas that the Hong Kong student seem inclined to avoid. Such resistance often points to an area of knowledge or a form of intellectual discipline that will enrich and balance the student's academic program. Skills, methods of inquiry, and knowledge often transfer across disciplines. The creative application of these in new contexts may lead to new insights or solutions. Moreover, the ability to analyze material critically from multiple perspectives may illustrate the limitations of any single theory, however powerful, in explaining a complex range of phenomena. Finally, breadth of study prepares the Hong Kong students to approach new questions not yet formulated, in fields and professions not yet imagined. Hence, it seems that when liberal studies subject becomes one essential subject to Hong Kong students, it will bring learning pressure and negative learning emotion to the Hong Kong students when they dislike this subject to study in Hong Kong high schools.

What are the elements of a Liberal Education ?

The original seven liberal arts, in the classical world, consisted of the trivium of deductive reasoning comprised of grammar, logic, and rhetoric, and the quadrivium of quantitative reasoning, which encompassed geometry, astronomy, arithmetic, and music. This liberal studies subject relates to natural philosophy (empirical science), moral philosophy (human thought and behavior), and metaphysics (ontology, or the study of being).

This liberal studies subject seems to an education in the natural sciences--biology, chemistry, physics, and psychology--introduces techniques of observation and experimentation, the relation of data to hypotheses, and the practice of scientific reasoning. This work trains the mind to relate concrete empirical information to abstract models, stimulating multidimensional and creative habits of thought. Sustained experience in the laboratory and a grasp of basic scientific principles lead to a better understanding of commonly observed phenomena. Nonspecialists who are scientifically literate bring valuable understanding to public discourse and to an increasing number of professional settings. It also teachs students how to make quantitative reasoning, with emphasis on mathematical models and methods above the secondary-school level, aids in the expression of hypotheses, processes, and theoretical relations. It seems that a course in statistics can be helpful for all students, and particularly for those who might work in the social and behavioral sciences. Studies in computer science offer valuable exposure to principles of logic and problem-solving paradigms. Moreover, it also teachs the study of human behavior and society leads students to investigate their own identities and to gain insight into social categories and relations. Faculty advisers often urge students to take a sustained look at the history of a specific society, and also to examine a contemporary society (or a segment of it) that is unfamiliar. In light of these encounters, students learn to make and evaluate their own political and ethical choices. Whether a student explores anthropology, economics, education, history, philosophy, political science, religious studies, sociology, or interdisciplinary studies, this question will lie near the heart of the inquiry: in what ways have people lived together, and how should they live together? However, liberal studies subject can train students skills to answer these any questions. Also, liberal studies students enlarge their understanding of the liberal arts through the study of creative expression. In the analysis of creative works, whether through historical survey of forms, aesthetic theory, or interpretive practice, the arts occupy the foreground, though knowledge of history and society may inform the analysis. In this way, courses in literature, music, theatre, dance, and the visual arts complement studies in anthropology, history, philosophy, religious studies, and other fields. Students also benefit from learning, through direct instruction in artistic or literary technique, the intense discipline of art and its interplay between conscious intent and unconscious design. Hence, students of the liberal arts should use this framework as a starting point for intellectual discovery and personal development as they plan their four years of study in consultation with their advisers.

U.S. Bureau of Labor Statistics (BLS) indicates that it was interesting to see that ten years after graduation, median salaries of students who attended elite liberal arts colleges are far lower than – as much as 50% lower, in some cases – those of students who graduated from equally selective research universities, according to the Wall Street Journal .and data from the U.S. Department of Education. According to a study by Forbes, it may be wiser to get no college degree at all than to spend four years and hundreds of thousands of dollars earning a humanities B.A. They found that a striking 64% of hiring managers said they would consider a candidate who hadn't gone to a day of college. At the same time, fewer than 2% of hiring managers said they were actively recruiting liberal arts grads.Now let's discuss, what really makes a liberal arts education useless? Well it's all the same reasons which make it so exceptional and divergent, or at least most of them.
What are the benefits liberal studies subject can bring benefits to students. Liberal arts programs provide students with a broad and general education that covers different areas of thought. However, these programs often do not provide a significant depth of experience and study in any one area. There may not be the opportunity to learn and develop any particular technical skills to a proficient level.

Liberal arts graduates then find themselves without the entry-level skills required for professional jobs, since they primarily divulge in the development of what may be referred to as, "soft skills". This includes courses that discuss the great instruction in cognitive ability, critical thinking skills, writing, and analysis and is without reference to any hard skills like computer programming,, designing any kind software or typing/writing.Even subjects that are based on post-modernist kind of theories, such as Gender studies, Sociology etc, are quite useless in terms of attaining a well paid job. Another example of an incessant major is one that prepares you for further education, such as political science, acting as a stepping stone for, perhaps, law school. It's also a matter of how much demand is actually there, in the job market, for a certain area of expertise. It is well known that there can never be enough IT people in the industry, however law students are often left in the cold, due to the great competition in the field. Thus, the disadvantages of a liberal arts education include lack of preparation for employment. There in no development of technical skills and real-world experience, which means that liberal arts students may still need to learn basic job skills outside of their courses to be marketable and employable.

It is important to understand that a liberal arts degree is likely to be quite expensive, placing one in debt upon graduation and affording one a non-existent economic advantage in the job marketplace. It is known that in the 20th century, one could easily enter a graduate program after their bachelors. However, now graduate schools require work experience, which is hard to attain when employers don't consider a liberal arts to be as significant as one with a technical background. Since funding for liberal arts education has also reduced, claiming other major subjects are much more likely to be effective employees. The entire objective of a college education is to get a job in a related field and earn a salary that justifies the cost of four years' worth of college tuition, liberal arts degrees are subject to a significant amount of public criticism for not being a wise investment. After all, compared to other majors, liberal arts majors on average make less and are more likely to be underemployed (in a job that doesn't require a bachelor's degree) right out of college.Therefore, the reason why many consider a liberal studies major degree to be more valuable could be due to the focus on developing technical and professional skills that are directly applicable to career-related positions. The skills acquired in a liberal arts degree program may be considered more abstract and less valuable in the short-term after graduation.

It is quite essential to understand that a broad knowledge may seem as an effective skill set for life but in terms of employment, one must maintain a certain specific skill set, so as to set themselves apart. The explosion of the information age makes the Liberal Arts seem irrelevant. There is no way to broadly educate students in a world so overrun by information, knowledge and rapid change; it merely dilutes the essence of everything they learn. Therefore, it is quite essential to understand that, a liberal arts education does not offer the required skills to it's students. Not only that, their expensive nature makes it exceedingly difficult for graduates to pay off loans, since their jobs tend to be on the lesser end of economic value. Therefore, in today's age and time, the nature of a liberal art degree doesn't hold much in terms of a fruitful career, regardless whatever personal skills may be developed.Today more than ever, it is critical for a serious-minded young person to avoid a worthless major in college. Huge numbers of college grads have discovered that their degrees were next to worthless, and went on to get the exact same low-paying service jobs that their parents threatened them with when they screwed around in high school.

I absolutely love to complain about worthless degrees, but I also believe that this liberal studies degree only one worth degree to US, but it may be one worthless degree to Hong Kong, because Hong Kong labor market has no much need for liberal studies major degree graduated students nowadays. My worthless degrees did nothing but remove me from the world of real work; to widen between myself and the actual jobs which existed in the real economy, such as Hong Kong is not one real suitable economic environment to need any liberal studies students' skills nowadays. In short, I didn't have the sort of skills that people were willing to pay for, and had to restart at temp jobs that I could have gotten straight out of high school.That is the problem of a "liberal" education to Hong Kong students. The point of education is - or at least should be - to make the world whole and comprehensible for the learncr through instruction, and to prepare the young for adulthood. Having a job is part of being an adult in the real world, and education which does nothing to provide for this is hardly education at all.

WHAT MAKES A DEGREE WORTHLESS to Hong Kong liberal studies major students? In the 1960's about 10-15 percent of the workforce had college degrees. Today, that number hovers at around 40 percent, and in the United States we have had a decade of virtually no economic growth. That entry-level job that allowed the English major to enter the white-collar workforce in 1970 doesn't exist anymore. A college degree is worthless if nobody is willing to pay you for the skills you acquired while earning it. Any art graduates, as well as those from Accounting programs, learned actual skills in their studies. Humanities majors learned only "soft skills" like writing, and "critical thinking." All useless majors teach the same "soft skills."

Many of the useful majors also teach them, so why not choose a useful major?

What does one useful major, such as liberal studies to Hong Kong students look like? It includes these factors to influence the liberal studies education implementation to Hong Kong students to learn successfully, they may include these factors as below:

1. It is all soft skills.

If the department only discusses the great instruction in cognitive ability, critical thinking skills, writing, and analysis and is without reference to any hard skills like running a computer, keeping the books, or designing a satellite; it is probably a worthless major.

2. It prepares you for graduate studies.

I was a Political Science major. It is a terrible major. It prepares you for law school, which is a graduate program that churns out about 3 graduates per available job in that field. That is all Poli-sci does. The ultimate soft skill is preparation for more school.

3. It contains absolutely no math

Mathematics is the language of the universe. Deal with it. Any major that has no arithmetic at all is likely to be a massive waste of time. It doesn't have to be calculus, but if you hardly ever add, subtract, divide, or multiply, your major is worthless.

4. The Bureau of Labor Statistics data on the field are terrible.

If there are no jobs in the field, or the starting salaries are lower than the median salaries of jobs that don't require a college degree, your major is a waste of time.

5. It's all for helping people, but it doesn't.

Liberal studies subject seems to sociology majors like to pretend that they're going to have a career in the non-profit sector where they will help people; usually by nagging people. Somehow, that's helpful. They end up working as part-time HR Generalists who reject job applicants for "not being a good fit." People with Nursing degrees help people by being nurses. Kindergarten teachers, and pharmacy techs also help people... by helping people.

6. SUPPLY AND DEMAND factor

Courses of study that are attached to an actual career track can become worthless if the number of graduates greatly exceeds the available number of jobs. The graduate program of Law is an example. TaxProf Blog: Looking at the Law School Crisis. Law in the United States has become something of an All-Purpose Liberal Arts graduate degree. The course material is entirely "soft skills," being focused on things like legal reasoning, critical thinking skills, and argumentation in the framework of the Socratic Method. With the possible exception of learning how to write a court brief, a law degree doesn't teach "hard skills."Those soft skills are necessary to successfully practice law. The problems happen when law schools blast out far too many graduates for the job market. Left out of the legal field, those graduates are forced to navigate a job market with what is essentially a Liberal Arts degree.

Electrical engineering is a good major. Mining engineering is as well. An AA in Computer Networking would also be a pretty good choice. Geology is probably a better major than Geography, which would be valuable on Jeopardy but not necessarily in the job market.

Accounting is probably a better choice than Finance, which is probably better than Economics, which is definitely better than Political Science, which is absolutely better than

Gender Studies. College is too expensive, and too time-consuming, to be entered with a whimsical disregard for the student's future in the real world. That is the hard truth of life, and hiding away in the collegiate land of Humanities make-believe will only make the eventual crash much more devastating.

A liberal arts education provides all of the fundamentals necessary to survive in a changing workplace. You take core classes in fields like sociology, anthropology, mathematics and science to build a foundation that prepares you for life in the real world. This type of education is meant to build a well-rounded student who not only is an expert in her chosen field, but also an excellent critical thinker and competent writer.

7.Class Size/Faculty Access factor

The liberal arts education provides a smaller, more personalized approach for your college experience. Class sizes are relatively small, allowing students access to professors and giving them the ability to interact with each other more, both in and out of the classroom. In a larger research university, classes may have up to 500 students in a lecture hall, and you typically don't have a relationship with the professor. University professors are under pressure to keep up with research trends and gain grants and national accreditation for the university, which leaves less time for the personal mentoring of undergraduate students.

8.Broad Versus Focused factor

Students receiving a liberal arts education have to take a broad range of classes, requiring them to learn not only about the subjects in their majors, but also about writing, critical thinking and mathematics. A liberal arts student who is a biology major also is takes classes in public speaking, composition and philosophy, giving those students the ability to write more comprehensive lab reports and communicate their research to an audience in an organized manner. A university student focuses more on the major area of study, taking more science classes that relate to the profession or intended graduate program.

9.Learning communication skill factor

A major disadvantage of a liberal arts education is the lack of funding available for cutting edge equipment and research materials. For example, science students at liberal arts colleges don't have access to the same expensive microscopes or computers as students at a university.. The library at a liberal arts college may not have the vast selection of old and new materials available for research. Universities draw in nationally recognized field experts who can teach students from their real life experiences and who have research funding to continue their studies. Liberal arts colleges have professors who have a great passion for their chosen field, but they may not have the same credentials or outside connections.

Communication skills are greatly valued in the workplace, and they can also increase your quality of life. In gaining a liberal arts education, you will learn to understand the characteristics of effective communication and the contextual factors that influence individuals. In today's world, having the ability to communicate professionally can benefit you in almost any field. If you enjoy building and maintaining relationships with others and want to incorporate this into your career, consider earning a degree in communications. With this degree, you can prepare to work as a writer, editor, public relations specialist, corporate trainer or human resources coordinator. With strong communication skills, the possibilities are endless!

10.Improving Critical Thinking Skills factor

In your liberal arts degree program, you will have the opportunity to practice and improve your critical thinking skills. What does it mean to think critically? Oftentimes, our thinking can tend to be biased, which can hinder us from making wise decisions. However, when we think critically, we assess situations by skillfully analyzing the problem at hand, taking all factors into consideration. In order to improve your critical thinking skills, the courses you take during your liberal arts education will encourage you to think about a wide variety of topics. You will work to assess problems and think critically in order to create solutions. Developing this skill can help you to succeed not only in your career, but also in life.

11. liberal studies can be one assist subject to raise students' learning interesting

The arts and science are often thought of as polar opposites. Traditionally, students and universities view them as separate entities – you pick a degree in one or the other and stick to your side of the fence.Increasingly though, this way of doing things is not enough to prepare students for the data-drenched and volatile workplace of the twenty-first century.

Combining arts and science in the curriculum could be the answer. From science, students learn about sound methods for testing hypotheses, and about interpreting and drawing valid conclusions from data. From arts, they will also learn about developing arguments, and about understanding, moving, and changing the minds of diverse audiences. There are double and combined degrees already on offer. But there is a great potential for them to be better

– improving students' employment prospects and fostering new skills in "the space between" speciality areas.

Double degree programs have significant untapped potential in preparing graduates for employment.The potential benefit, they argue, is that graduates develop "transdisciplinary skills" that are highly valued by employers. Transdisciplinary thinkers take a unique approach to solving problems. They draw information from diverse sources and seek collaborations to produce "socially robust knowledge". However, the way most combined and double degrees are established does not foster transdisciplinary learning.

This is because the combination of degrees tends to create an administrative rather than pedagogical structure. This means that an arts-science student, for example, simply has access to subjects from arts and science faculties. Upon graduation, graduates would be able to perform skills essential to both speciality areas. But they have not necessarily developed transdisciplinary thinking.

The rare double degrees that are pedagogically designed can unlock the potential of a combined curriculum. In such cases, arts-science graduates can also imaginatively develop unique research methods, or ethically interpret information systems, or persuade non-experts to change their behaviour based on scientifically informed debate.

Universities are increasingly considering different degree structures. The Australian National University (ANU) claims that their new flexible degrees improve graduate employability in a way that "suits your head and your heart". Students complete any two degrees in four years from arts, social sciences, business, or science. The University of Sydney offers a similar option with a four-year Bachelor of Science and Arts.

Such degrees expedite a student's completion. But they are administrative combinations that rarely push students to experiment with approaches and practices from both degrees.

Employers repeatedly point to the complex nature of the modern work environment and advise that they highly value graduates with the skills provided by a broad general education. Some countries education policy need students must complete between two and four subjects from outside their faculty. For example, a science graduate must have completed subjects taught by non-science faculties, such as education, arts, business, built environment, or law. Such a program appears to be more pedagogically driven than the standard double degree. Students in "GenEd" subjects draw on their existing knowledge to solve problems in unfamiliar disciplinary locations. The learning promoted here is a valuable kind of creative disciplinarity, but it is not transdisciplinary.

We coordinate a new degree at the University of Sydney which has been designed to promote transdisciplinarity. The three-year Bachelor of Liberal Arts and Science (BLAS) offers students the administrative freedom to study in two faculties while mandating the completion of core units in critical thinking, ethics, and communication. Hence, BLAS students complete a major in arts or science, including up to 12 subjects in their chosen field. A further six to eight subjects are chosen from the other faculty. That is, an arts major must also complete six to eight science subjects. Finally, six liberal studies subjects must also be completed. Here in the physical and intellectual space of liberal studies subjects students from diverse disciplinary backgrounds collaborate to address problems of research, writing and ethics.task of developing global awareness to social studies courses, or should we spread the responsibility throughout the entire curriculum.

Reference

Curriculum development council (2001) learning to learn: lifelong learning and whole person development, Hong Kong: printing department.

Nussbaum, Martha Craven. Cultivating Humanity : A Classical Defense of Reform in Liberal Education. Cambridge, Mass.:Harvard University Press, 1997.

Paris, D and Kimball, BA (2000) Liberal education : An overlapping pragmatic consensus' Jounral of curriculum studies, 32 (2): 143-58.

Source: *U.S. Bureau of Labor Statistics (BLS)

www.ingramcontent.com/pod-product-compliance
Ingram Content Group UK Ltd.
Pitfield, Milton Keynes, MK11 3LW, UK
UKHW040004200726
13854UKWH00001B/38

9 798887 041001